The
Great
American
Amusement
Parks

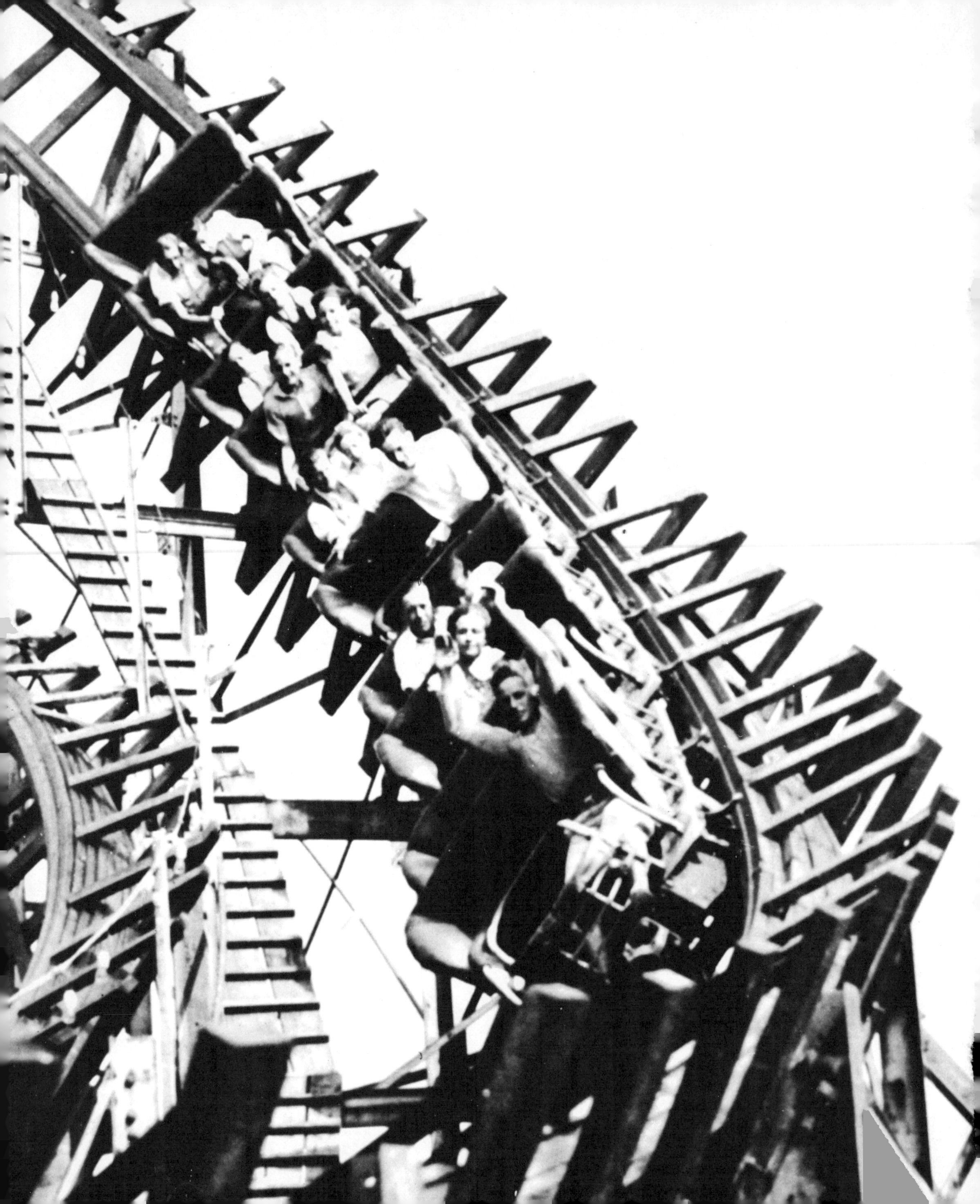

THE GREAT AMERICAN AMUSEMENT PARKS A PICTORIAL HISTORY BY GARY KYRIAZI

CASTLE BOOKS

Arrangement has been made to publish this edition
by Castle Books, a division of
Book Sales Inc. of Secaucus, New Jersey

Manufactured in the United States of America

June — 1978

Library of Congress Cataloging in Publication Data

Kyriazi, Gary.
The Great American Amusement Parks.

Includes index.
1. Amusement parks—History. I. Title.
GV1851.A35K97   790'.068   76-2475
ISBN 0-8065-0525-7

To my Daddy,
who put me on my first roller coaster
when I was three years old

Acknowledgments

The author expresses his sincere gratitude to the following parks, organizations, and individuals whose help proved invaluable to the creation of this book:

Mr. Robert H. Blundred, Executive Secretary, International Association of Amusement Parks and Attractions, Oak Park, Illinois.

Miss Christine L. Bogomaz, San Diego, California.

Crystal Beach Transit Company, Buffalo, New York.

Geauga Lake Park, Aurora, Ohio.

Hersheypark, Hershey, Pennsylvania.

Mr. and Mrs. Carl O. Hughes, Kennywood Park, West Mifflin, Pennsylvania.

Idora Park, Youngstown, Ohio.

Kings Island, Kings Mills, Ohio.

Lagoon Corporation, Salt Lake City, Utah.

Los Angeles County Museum of Natural History, Los Angeles, California.

Mr. James A. Payer, San Francisco, California.

Santa Cruz Seaside Company, Santa Cruz, California.

Mr. Frederick Schumacher, Lake Havasu, Arizona.

Mr. Kenneth Strickfaden, Los Angeles, California.

Westchester County Playland Commission, Rye, New York.

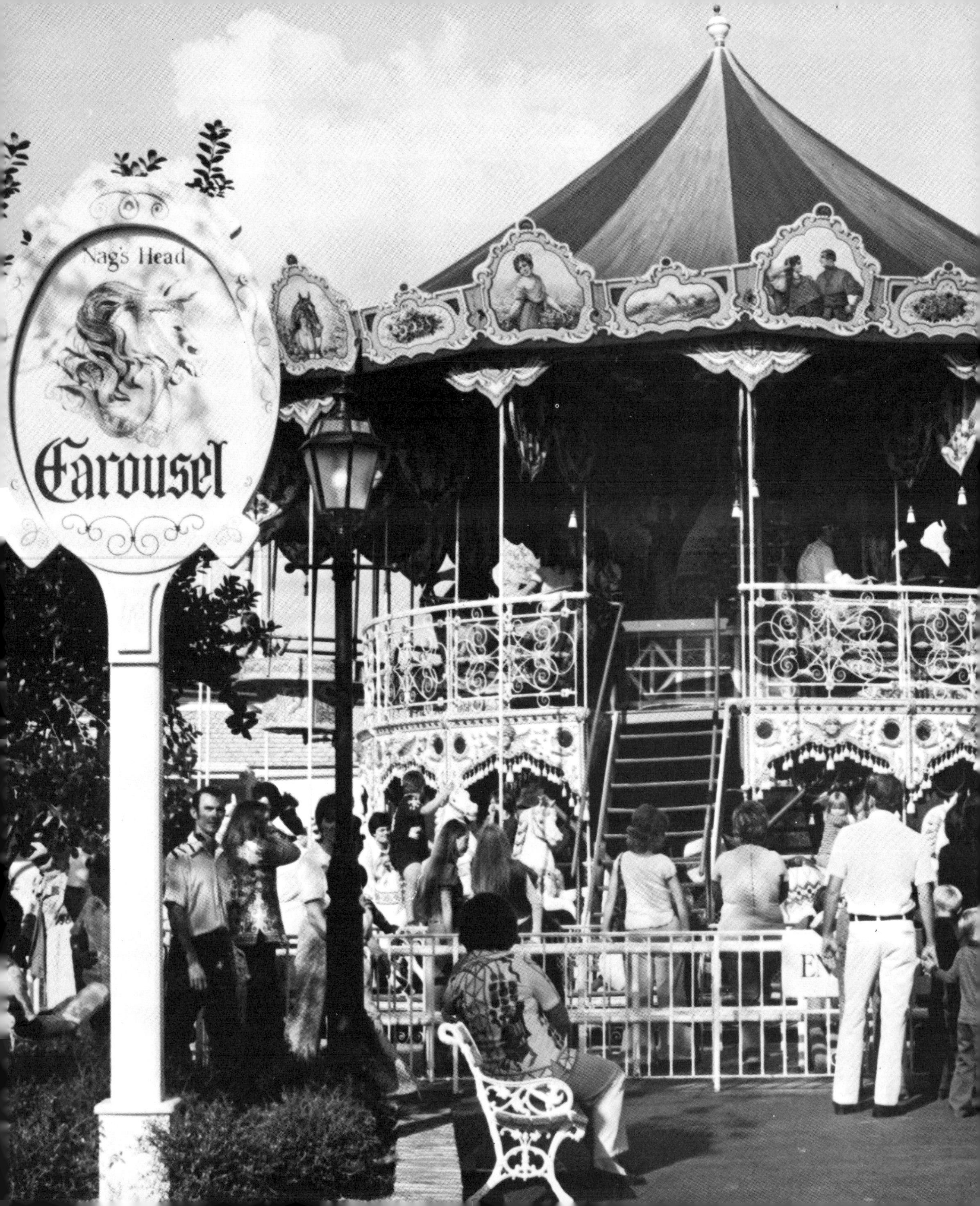
Nag's Head
Carousel

Mathew Wallace Rosecrans

Contents

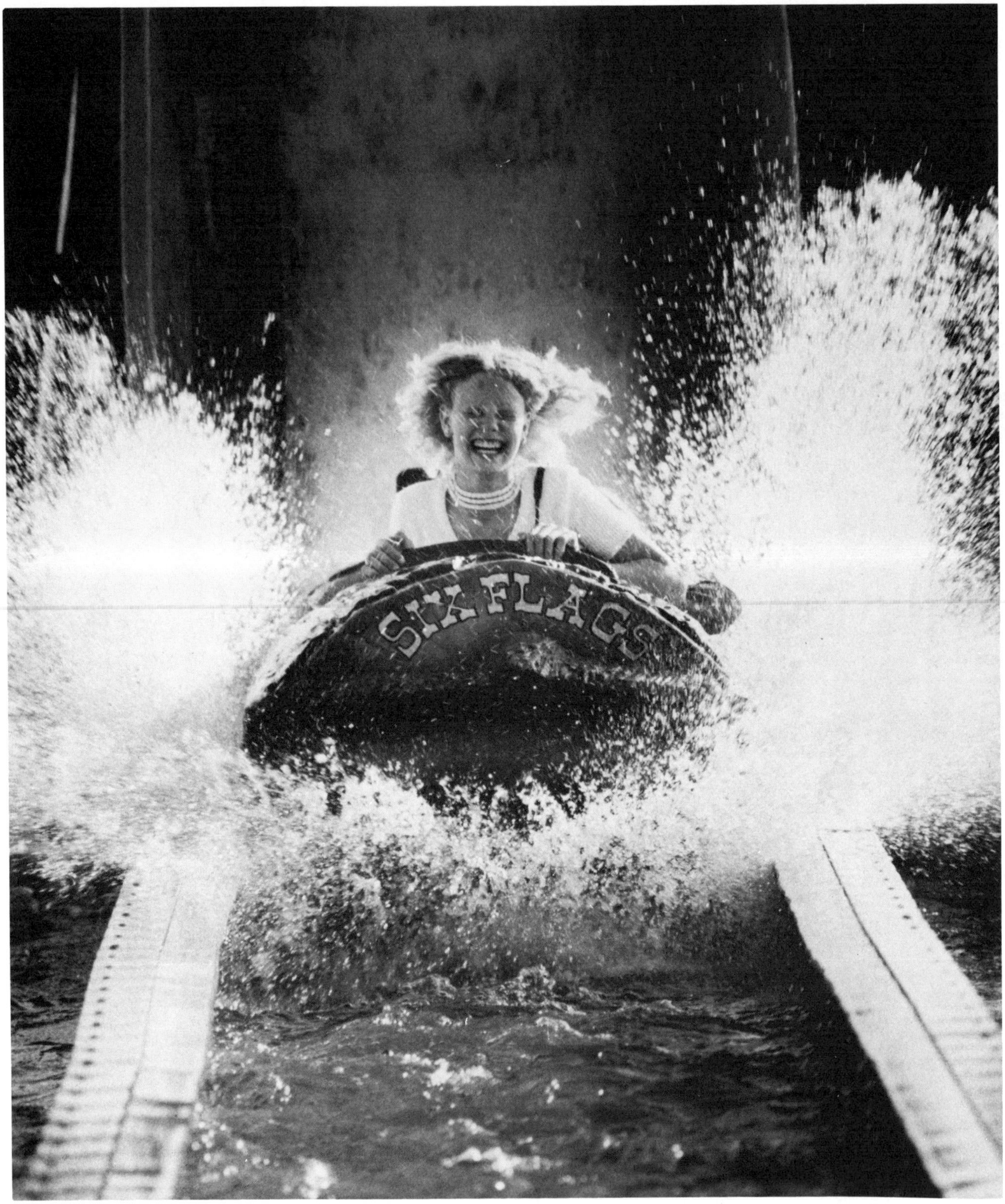
SIX FLAGS

Introduction

THERE IS SOMETHING in all of us that is always trying to break free of the everyday existence which seems to become more sedate and staid as we grow older. The child inside us is always crying to be let loose from our adult surroundings, making the businessman fight the impulse to leave his desk and go outside to play in the nearest mud puddle, or tempting the housewife to put down her mop and go outside to play hopscotch.

The drive for fun and diversion from everyday reality is as old as man. Many believe that the cave paintings of the Stone Age were meant chiefly for the caveman's own entertainment, so that he could live out the dreams and fantasies which took him away from the daily chore of hunting for food. As man became more civilized, so his needs for entertainment became stronger and more diversified. The Roman Empire probably took one of the first and biggest steps in mass entertainment with its construction of coliseums and its presentations of the "games," including the barbaric but always crowd-pleasing gladiatorial games, slave auctions, and, later, persecution of the Christians.

But just as the wealth and abundance of the Roman Empire had created the time for its citizens to enjoy such "entertainment," its eventual breakdown sent the Romans back out into the fields to a sunup-to-sundown fight for survival. This type of existence was to continue for Western man throughout the Middle Ages until the rise of the middle class, the establishment of towns and commerce and, later, the Industrial Revolution spread throughout most of Europe in the sixteenth, seventeenth, and eighteenth centuries. There was now more time to spare, time to indulge in carefree activity and entertainment. Shakespeare's plays were filling the theaters in England with large, enthusiastic audiences, the bullrings in Spain were filled with hoarsely cheering crowds, while in France people were enjoying the beginnings of what would eventually become one of America's greatest institutions—the amusement park.

Chapter One
The Evolution
of the
Amusement Park

IN THE SEVENTEENTH CENTURY, large parks known as "pleasure gardens" began spreading throughout France and soon most of Europe. Visitors at these gardens could spend warm summer afternoons and evenings enjoying a large array of sports and activities which included bowling, tennis, shuffleboard, ringing, and sharpshooting. The parks were interlaced with fountains, flower beds, and tree-lined paths where people could stroll and relax, and several food and drink stands were available serving cold and refreshing novelties. Bright and colorful lighting was used during the evenings, and this was a source of entertainment in itself to most people, who were used to spending their evenings in dimly lit homes.

By the beginning of the eighteenth century, as pleasure gardens became more popular, the variety of entertainment began to increase as circus acts presented feats such as tightrope and trapeze acts. Balloon ascensions became extremely popular, and

A French pleasure garden with a primitive Ferris wheel and an ancestor of the roller coaster, c. 1800.

Vauxhall Gardens during its peak, showing the bandstand in the center, the refreshments area to the left, and the game and spectacle area at the rear of the gardens.

several parks began presenting a new and rather dangerous spectacle known as parachute jumping. A short time later, music became an integral part of pleasure gardens, as instrumental and vocal concerts performed. Social dancing—considered sinful by English Puritanism—became one of the more popular attractions in the gardens. Gambling began to appear at some pleasure gardens, which in turn became known as the less reputable of the pleasure gardens, as prostitution and liquor consumption in quantity began to join the gambling.

Unlike the French pleasure gardens, which began mainly as gardens, the English pleasure gardens were usually an outgrowth of an inn or tavern. One of these, the Vauxhall Gardens in London, became the first internationally famous pleasure garden when it opened in 1661. There was no admission charge to enter the gardens; visitors paid only for the entertainments and amusements they enjoyed once they were inside. In 1728 a one-shilling admission was established. Vauxhall Gardens enjoyed great popularity, and visitors came from all over the Continent to enjoy the sports, activities,

Evening dancing in Vauxhall Gardens.

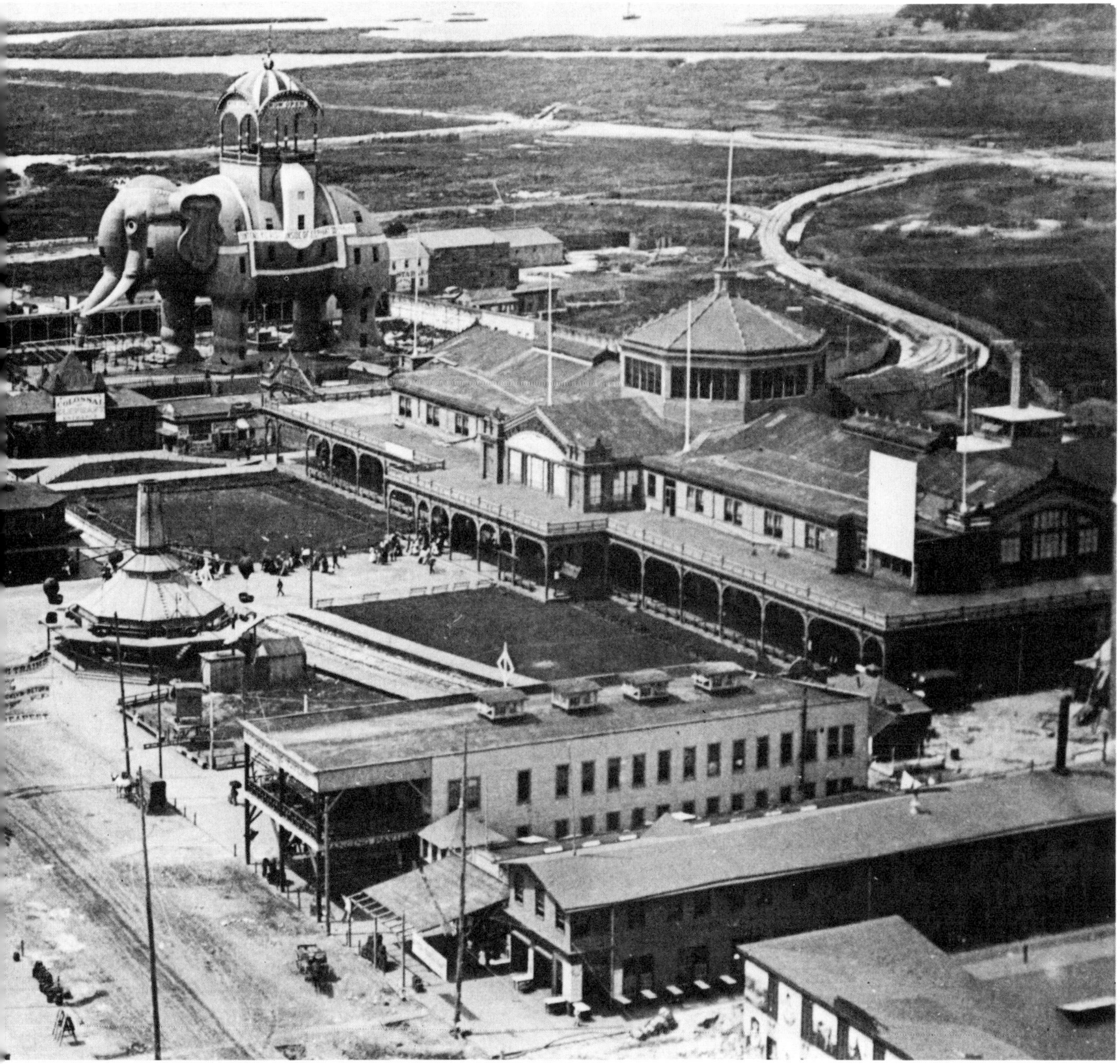
COLOSSAL

*Dining in Charles Feltman's
Ocean Pavilion in the 1920s.
The hot dog was "unfit."*

*The prices at Nathan's
Famous were still low in
1939. Twenty-five cents
bought a nice meal. (Museum
of the City of New York)*

Coney's rustic beginnings: Peter Tilyou's Surf House in 1874. (Brooklyn Public Library)

west end of the island with Sheepshead Bay on the east, separating Coney from Brooklyn. But storms and man's bridges and footpaths eventually put an end to the creek, and today it is impossible to find even a trace of it.

The sand dunes of Coney remained relatively undisturbed until 1829, when the first shell road was built and the first beach hotel, the Coney Island House, was constructed. By the 1840s, the Coney Island House was famous as a summer vacation hotel, and its many guests included Herman Melville, Edgar Allan Poe, Jenny Lind, P. T. Barnum, Daniel Webster, Henry Clay, and Washington Irving. Walt Whitman was a frequent visitor, and he would spend most of the day in solitude on, as he later wrote, "the long, bare, unfrequented shore, which I had all to myself, and where I loved, after bathing, to race up and down the hard sand, and declaim Homer or Shakespeare to the surf and seagulls by the hour."

But the peace and solitude wasn't going to last for long. Because of the east-west direction of the beach, the sun shines directly on Coney Island all day long, providing excellent weather for sun and surf bathing. Ocean bathing was a new and curious sport to the New Yorkers, who began visiting Coney in ever-increasing numbers to frolic in the sand and surf.

By 1850, Coney Island was becoming widely talked about as a pleasant and quiet summer resort, and the crowds were coming so often that a plank road was constructed to accommodate them. A few months later, a pavilion was constructed stretching out over the water, and on throughout the 1860s the beach began steadily building with more pavilions, hotels, bathhouses and beer halls.

One of these was the huge Iron Pier, which stretched into the Atlantic for 1,000 feet. It offered various games, dancing, food, and it contained 1,200 bath lockers. The famous Iron Steamboat began making regular trips from Manhattan to the Iron Pier. When the first railroad to Coney was built in the 1870s and the daily visitors numbered in excess of 50,000, business and enterprise began overflowing the island.

Quick to become the most popular enterprises on Coney at this time were the several pavilions that lined the shore, most of them within 200 or 300 yards of the high-water mark. They were simple constructions consisting basically of a flat pier with a toadstool type of ceiling. Later pavilions had walls on one, two, or three sides to protect their guests from the ocean elements. Cabaret entertainment was popular in these pavilions, with the number-one audience pleaser, a female singer with powerful lungs who could belt out sad, heartfelt ballads. The highly receptive audiences would applaud loudly for such an act while seated in tables and chairs around the stage area, drinking the wine or beer offered by the house.

Some pavilions offered vaudeville, slapstick, and melodrama, and many of them had various games, carousels, clay duck shooting, gypsy fortunetellers, and guess-your-age-and-weight concessions. There were still other theaters, not along the ocean, that

The Iron Tower, c. 1900. It burned down in the Dreamland fire of 1911. (James A. Payer Collection)

L. A. Thompson's Switchback Railway, 1884.

Scenic railways were the thrill of the day in 1886. People loved to pretend they were dangerous. (Museum of the City of New York)

Scenic railways took on all shapes and forms. This L. A. Thompson Scenic Railway at the San Francisco Pan-Pacific Exposition of 1915 used the elephant as its come-on.

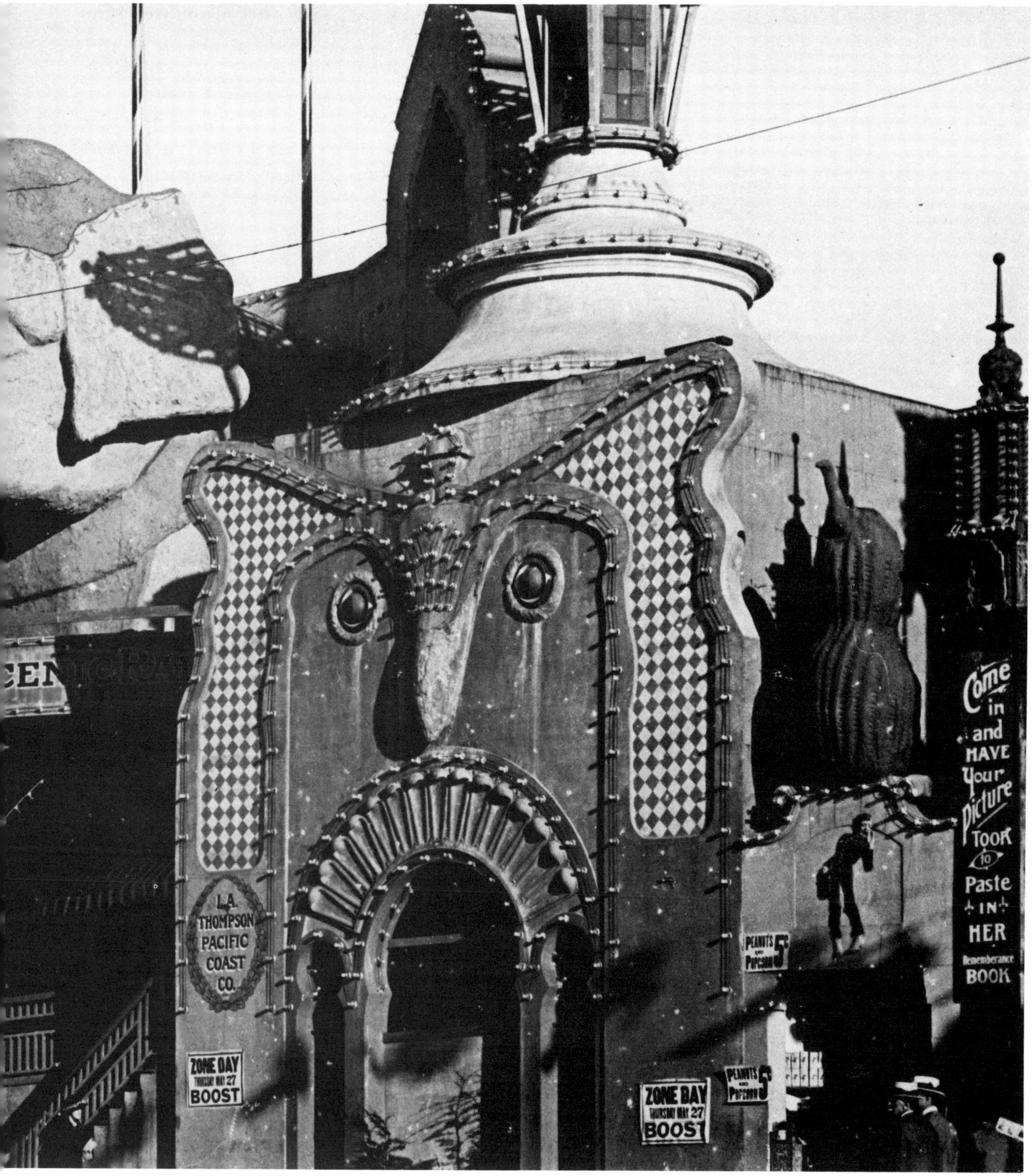
L.A. THOMPSON PACIFIC COAST CO.
ZONE DAY THURSDAY MAY 27 BOOST
ZONE DAY THURSDAY MAY 27 BOOST
PEANUTS AND POPCORN 5¢
PEANUTS AND POPCORN 5¢
Come in and HAVE Your Picture TOOK TO Paste IN HER Rememberance BOOK

presented more questionable entertainment and diversions, and were no more than opium dens and houses of prostitution. The area of Coney which during the 1850s and 1860s abounded in sin in all of its forms was appropriately called the Gut, a grouping of huts and shanties located between what later became West 1st and West 3rd Streets.

Fortunately the Gut represented only a tiny fraction of Coney Island, and in the 1870s it was overshadowed by the emergence of several high-class hotels patterned after the manner set by the Coney Island House. These hotels began a competition in luxury and aristocratic pull which ushered in Coney Island's "Elegant Era." The first of the huge grand hotels was Charles Feltman's Ocean Pavilion.

Young Charles Feltman had been doing a fairly good business as a pie vendor in the early 1860s, taking advantage of the throngs of New Yorkers who were discovering Coney Island. On one particularly slow afternoon in 1867, Feltman was wondering what original food concoction he could invent that would catch the public's fancy and sell profitably, and possibly replace the clam as Coney's food specialty. On a whim, he put a Vienna sausage into a kaiser roll and took a bite. He chewed slowly, wondering, then added some mustard and took another bite. After his enthusiasm was shared by some friends, Charles began selling his "red hots," as he dubbed them, faster than he could make them. As it goes with anything new and wildly popular, speculation and jealous attention was raised about these new red hots. One newspaper article questioned the contents of the meat used in red hots, suggesting that it could be dog meat, and thus the American hot dog was born.

The Cyclone was owned and operated for several years by Chris Fuerst and George Kister, whose close adherence to the strict maintenance and operation required of roller coasters is responsible for the Cyclone's safe history. (Brooklyn Public Library)

The "Flying Turns" coaster was bought from the New York World's Fair
of 1939 by Steeplechase Park. The ride burned down in 1956.
(Brooklyn Public Library)

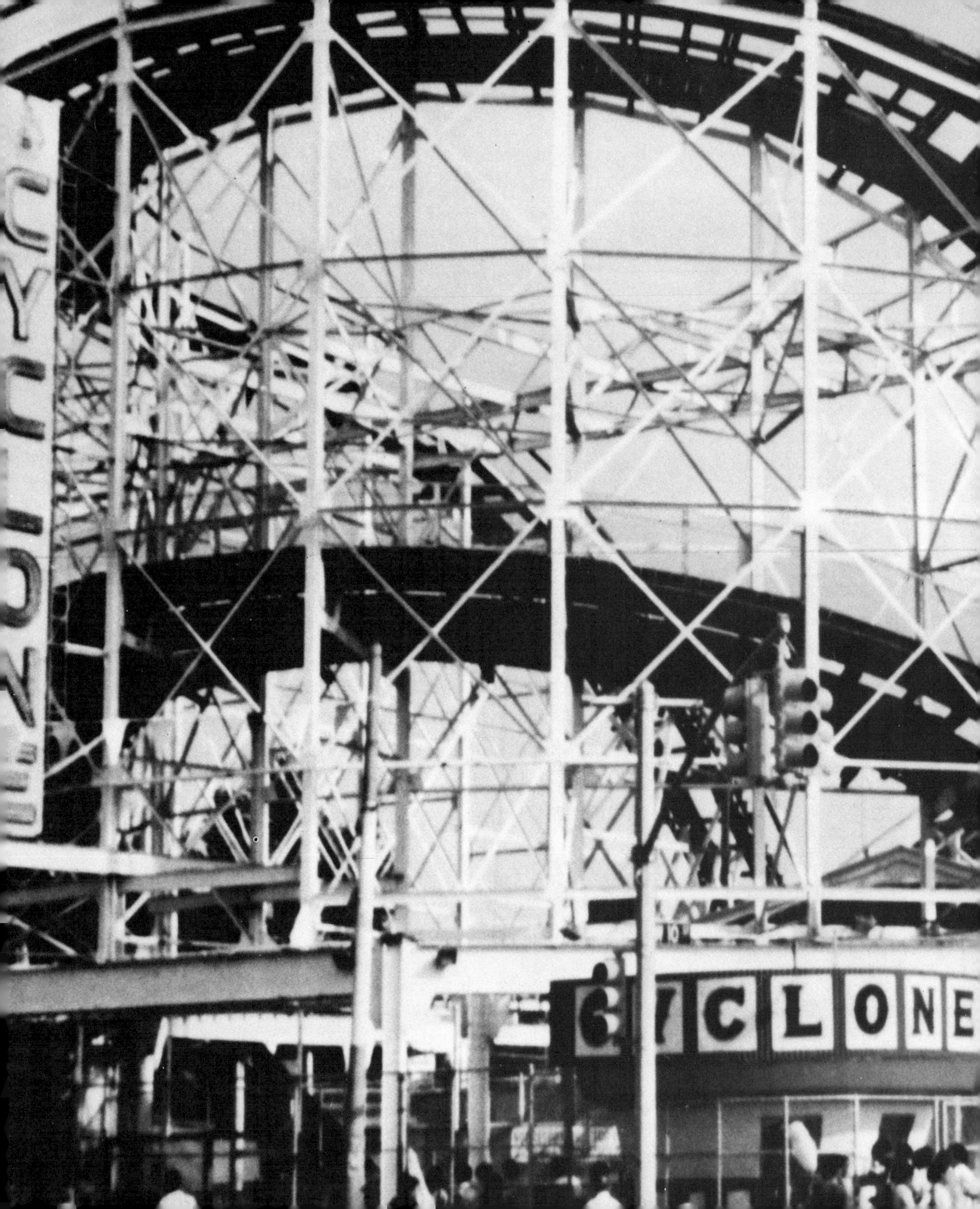
CYCLONE

The "Cyclone," located at Surf Avenue and West 10th.

The "Tickler" was located in Luna Park.
(Brooklyn Public Library)

With his hot dog success, Feltman became a very rich man almost overnight, and in 1874 he built the magnificent Charles Feltman's Ocean Pavilion. The hotel's lavish rooms held 20,000 guests, who dined in elegance and danced in a ballroom big enough for 3,000 dancers, and was lit by 11 electric lights and 400 gas jets. The Ocean Pavilion's restaurant became the biggest and best restaurant on Coney Island. It could serve 8,000 people in a pleasant atmosphere of beautiful gardens and soft music. There was Bavarian beer on tap, but the hot dog was left out. Feltman believed that the hot dog was unfit for the elegance of the Ocean Pavilion, and besides, there were dozens of hot dog stands on the island by that time.

In 1915, a young man named Nathan Handwerker opened a hot dog stand he called "Nathan's Famous," beginning his own Coney Island monopoly on hot dogs by selling them at a nickel each, instead of the standard ten cents. Today, Nathan's Famous is still in operation at Coney Island as the biggest hot dog emporium in the world, with a large and tasty bill of fare that includes corn on the cob, pizza, shrimp, clams, beer on tap, and a delicatessen.

During Nathan's five-cent era (hot dogs are now fifty cents), many people found they could eat quite cheaply by taking their breakfasts, lunches, and dinners at Nathan's, until, of course, they lost their appetite for hot dogs. The man who to this day holds the Coney Island record for hot dog eating is the New York Yankees' Babe Ruth, who ate two dozen hot dogs at one sitting, washed down with a gallon of lemonade.

Following the success of Feltman's Ocean Pavilion, the Manhattan Beach Hotel was built in 1876, far out on the eastern shore of Coney, and for thirty years it was the most fashionable resort hotel in the U.S. Its lavish rooms, restaurants, shops, and ballrooms were lacking in nothing, and it presented spectacular entertainment that

Ready for departure on the Tickler, 1908.
(Museum of the City of New York)

included huge fireworks displays which pictured scenic wonders, famous legends, and battles.

The Manhattan Beach Hotel was quickly followed in 1878 by the Brighton Beach Hotel, which featured champagne on draft, and in 1879 by the Sea Beach Palace. When the Oriental Hotel was built in 1880, its beautifully ornate architecture seemed to be the last word in elegance, but it was surpassed in 1882 when James V. Lafferty built The Elephant.

The Elephant—"The Colossus of Architecture"—was a hotel in the shape of an elephant. It stood 122 feet high, with legs that were 60 feet in circumference. One front leg housed a cigar store, and the other featured a diorama. Visitors and hotel guests entered The Elephant by way of a spiral staircase up one hind leg and exited down another staircase in the other hind leg. Above, The Elephant housed a shopping mall and several guest rooms, and its head, facing the ocean, served as a vista room.

The Elephant Hotel marked the beginning of the elephant's becoming the unofficial symbol of the American amusement park. A figure of an elephant appeared in almost every park in one way or another. It has long been a mystery why the American public was so fascinated with the elephant, and many psychologists claimed it was an expression of America's repressed sexuality. Whatever it was, the fad continued, at least in the amusement parks, on throughout the 1920s.

As people began flocking to Coney just to take a look at The Elephant, suddenly the face and atmosphere of Coney Island began to change. The absurdity (and again, mysterious fascination) of a huge tin-skinned elephant seemed to touch the funny bone of Coney Island, and what has been called the "Coney Island Lunacy," the never-ending laughter and gaiety, began to set in. Certainly Coney was still a vacation resort; it did

The Top of the Human Toboggan Slide.

Lifting Car Off the Rails Onto Friction Beams.

"Hitting the Pipe." Exit at the Bowl.

The Bottom of the Human Toboggan Slide. Made of Rattan.

THE MECHANICAL JOYS OF CONEY ISLAND.

The August 15, 1908, edition of Scientific American *featured a mechanical
study of Coney Island's many rides. (Courtesy* Scientific American)

have America's three biggest and most successful racetracks—Gravesend, Sheepshead
Bay, and Brighton Beach—and the 10,000 seat Coney Island Athletic Club was the
world's capital of boxing. But the visitors in the 1880s began coming to be entertained
and amused, and the amusement-park side of Coney Island began.

The first big Coney Island "amusement" had been brought to Coney in 1877 from
the Philadelphia Centennial Exposition. It was the Sawyer Observatory, renamed the
Iron Tower, standing 300 feet high. Two elevators took spectators to the top of the

The "Mountain Torrent." An Aqueous Ride.

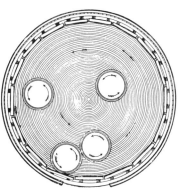

Diagram of the "Scrambler," Showing Direction of Rotation.

The "Scrambler." A Circular Rotating Floor Causes the Cars to Spin and Carom.

The "Tickler." An Inclined Plane Down Which Circular Cars Mounted on Casters Carom.

The "Arkansaw Traveler." Each Track Moves Independently, to the Sorrow of Many Would-be Travelers.

A Third-Rail Mountain Coaster Taking a Dip.

tower where a telescope enabled them to see out 40 miles. It afforded a magnificent view of New York City and much of the surrounding area.

Otherwise, amusements were sparse at Coney, and were generally limited to those types offered in the pavilions. But in 1884, a ride was presented on Coney which began a flourish of thrill rides of all kinds which has not ended to this day. LaMarcus Adna Thompson built and began operating what he named the Switchback Railway, the forerunner of what is still the king of all amusement rides, the roller coaster.

LaMarcus Thompson was a Sunday-school teacher from Philadelphia who was becoming concerned with young people frequenting beer gardens for their fun and entertainment. In his desire to create a cleaner source of outdoor amusement, Thompson stumbled upon the idea for his Switchback Railway. He had been intrigued by the success of an enterprising young Philadelphian who was making a small fortune by charging admission for rides in the mine cars of an abandoned coal mine. People were lining up by the hundreds to pay five cents to ride in the swift, small coal cars which cruised up, down, and around the old coal mining area.

Thompson's Switchback Railway was a simple affair. Passengers would board a car holding ten people. The car would then take off from the platform, making a straight-line course of gentle dips and rises until it came to rest at a station about 450 feet away. There the passengers would unload and climb to the top of the station, while a couple of strong attendants pushed the car up to the 30-foot top. The passengers would board again and enjoy another similar thrill back to the original starting place. The success of this simple yet clever device brought Thompson grosses of $700 a day, at five cents from customers who stood in line for hours for a ride.

In 1886 Thompson built the first fully developed roller coaster at Atlantic City. He named it the Oriental Scenic Railway. In this ride the loaded cars were automatically hauled to the top of the incline before set free under gravity. Halfway through the ride, the car ducked into a dark tunnel where it tripped a light switch that revealed picturesque scenes of the Orient painted on the walls. This tunnel part of the ride became extremely popular with the crowds, especially young couples, for whom the tunnel gave a chance for a quick embrace and a kiss. Thrills plus intimacy became the two important ingredients for a successful roller coaster.

Roller coasters quickly began springing up at Coney and all over the U.S., each new coaster trying to outdo all the rest in height, length, speed, and thrills. The speeds went from five miles per hour to over sixty, and the gentle 4-foot dips of Thompson's scenic railways became 100-foot nearly vertical plunges. Sharply banked turns were added, tunnels were placed in strategic places along the wildly designed track, and where there was no tunnel to provide intimacy, a sharp, fast turn would take its place by practically forcing a couple into each other's laps. Later, racing coasters became popular, as two coaster cars simultaneously released from the loading station would race side by side on a double track from start to finish, adding all the more excitement to the ride.

One of the biggest and best roller coasters, the Cyclone, was built at Coney in 1928 at a cost of $175,000. It is still operating today at a fee of one dollar a ride. Its owners are proud of telling the story of how the Cyclone cured a West Virginia coal miner named

Sea Lion Park in 1900. In the right foreground is the trained animal arena, to the left is the "Flip-Flap," and in the rear are the "Shoot-the-Chutes" and the lagoon where Captain Boyton performed his aquatic feats.

Emilio Franco of aphonia, a hysterical affliction which made him unable to speak. At the suggestion of his doctor of a possible roller-coaster cure, Franco doubtfully boarded the Cyclone, and after the ninety-second stomach-churning ride, he stumbled out of the car and said, "I feel sick." He almost was, too, when he realized he had talked.

The realization of the success of outdoor amusement rides led to a flourish of rides of all kinds which began scattering through Coney from the beginning of the 1890s on, with names like the Tickler, the Virginia Reel, Witching Waves, the Scrambler, Helter Skelter, Tumble Bug, Caterpillar, and the Human Toboggan Slide. Coney Island visitors spent money freely and gaily, discovering new ways they could be spun, bounced, jostled, frightened, and thrown into each other's laps, amidst helpless laughter and cries for more. An amused writer named P. G. Wodehouse wrote of the Coney Island experience:

> The principle at the bottom of Coney Island's success is the eminently sound one that what would be a brutal assault, if administered gratis, becomes a rollicking pleasure when charged for at the rate of fifteen cents per assault. Suppose one

Shooting-the-Chutes in Sea Lion Park, 1900. (New York Public Library)

laid hand upon you and put you in a large tub; suppose he then proceeded to send the tub spinning down an incline so arranged that at intervals of a few feet it spun around and violently bumped into something. Next day he would hear from your lawyer. But in Coney Island you jump into the Tickler and enjoy it; you have to enjoy it because you have paid good money to do so. Being in America, Coney Island is thought a little vulgar; if it were in France we would have written how essentially refined the Tickler and the Human Roulette Wheel were, and with what abundance and polish the French people took its pleasure.

"Old mills," or "tunnels-of-love," began vying with the roller coaster as the most popular rides, as couples would ride boats through dark, quiet waterways, occasionally getting a glimpse of a scene, but mostly staying in the dark. The water was kept flowing by a large waterwheel located at the entrance of the ride as an eye-catcher. One of the old mills at Coney was called the Fallen Angel, and at its entrance was a mannequin

The Flip-Flap in Sea Lion Park, 1900. (New York Public Library)

scene in which three nude girls glanced down in pity at a fourth girl lying on the ground, the "fallen angel." The scene created a fantastic business for the ride until the police insisted that the figures be clothed, which caused the ride's attendance to drop considerably.

While there were dozens of rides crowding Coney by 1894, there was no grouping of them, each being operated as a private concession by its owner. The season at Coney lasts from Memorial Day weekend until Labor Day, and concessionaires—be they ride, food, sideshow, or whatever—have to make their year's wages in this time. If the weather is good for most of the season, a nice profit can be made, but bad weather can mean financial ruin.

The various landowners of Coney would rent out their land in leases which would usually last from sometime in the early spring through Labor Day. To protect themselves from renters who would slip their lease when a season proved to be a bad one, landlords asked for the rent to be paid in three installments: one upon signing the lease, the second installment on Memorial Day, and the third on the Fourth of July. If the balance of the summer season yielded bad weather, the rent was already collected and the individual lessee took the loss.

Captain Paul Boyton came up with the idea of grouping rides and attractions into a single, enclosed amusement park with an admission fee charged at the gate. On the Fourth of July in 1895, he opened Sea Lion Park on Coney Island directly behind the Elephant Hotel. It became Coney Island's, the nation's, and the world's first enclosed amusement park.

While Paul Boyton was a relative newcomer to Coney, he was already famous as the world's first frogman, swimming across the English Channel and other large bodies of water in his self-invented inflated rubber suit. He became an international celebrity with his aquatic feats, and his navigation of several of the world's major rivers, including a 450-mile trip down the Rhine. In 1896 he began traveling around the world presenting his aquatic circus, in which he starred in the stunt-filled aqua show, in addition to his trained juggling sea lions. Boyton eventually decided to settle his circus in one place, and that is what led him to the construction and opening of his Sea Lion Park, the forerunner of the several marine-life parks which are so successful today.

Boyton and his forty sea lions were the top-billed attraction of Sea Lion Park, supported by an old mill, the "Cages of Wild Wolves," and a large ballroom. But an original ride called the Shoot-the-Chutes quickly became the park's most popular attraction. The Shoot-the-Chutes was an aquatic ride in which flat-bottomed boats holding a dozen passengers raced down a long, watery slide to a splashy end in a large lagoon. This ride became so successful that Boyton soon opened up Shoot-the-Chutes in Chicago, Washington, Boston, and San Francisco. Eventually old mills and Shoot-the-Chutes were combined to make the popular mill chute ride, an old mill that featured as its climax a 30-foot climb in the dark, leading to a 30-foot drop down into an open lagoon. Mill chutes were to be found in virtually every major amusement park in the country, and there are several still in operation today.

Another curious new attraction in Sea Lion Park was the Flip-Flap, invented by Lina Beecher. This ride was a roller coaster in which a small car holding two passengers coasted down an incline at a high speed and traveled in a complete overhead loop 25 feet in diameter, after which it coasted on into the station. This upside-down head-over-heels ride attraction stirred interest, but it had an unpleasant side effect. Riders found that they received a sharp jerk and strain while entering the loop, causing a mild whiplash. As these pain-in-the-neck complaints mounted, the management installed high-back chairs in the little car, but the customers still reported their pains. Eventually the ride was dismantled.

A better centrifugal force coaster was erected on Coney in 1901. This was the famous Loop-the-Loop coaster designed by Edward Prescott. Prescott found the formula which changed the failure of the Flip-Flap into success: he made the loop on his Loop-the-Loop an ellipse, rather than the true circular form of the Flip-Flap. The Loop-the-Loop was an immediate hit and an engineering victory. It received nationwide newsreel publicity in which a public demonstration showed that a glass of water placed in the car would not spill a drop as it executed the loop. Many people paid admission just to enter the area so they could watch the less fearful ride the loop.

LOOP THE LOOP

The Greatest Sensation of the Age

THE SAFEST AND THE GREATEST ATTRACTION

NO DANGER WHATEVER

Your vist will not be complete until you ride on the famous Loop the Loop

This advertisement for the "Loop-the-Loop" appeared in a Coney Island brochure in 1905. (Museum of the City of New York)

The Loop-the-Loop had more watchers than riders. The sign on the fence reads "Beware of Pickpockets." (James A. Payer Collection)

But the success of any amusement ride depends on an interesting paradox which only the most talented ride designers can achieve: the ride must look extremely dangerous to the public, and yet the public must be convinced the ride is completely safe. The Loop-the-Loop easily won the first half on looking dangerous, but the public would not believe that it was safe, even though in reality the ride was flawless. But even if the public had been convinced the Loop-the-Loop was safe, it would have failed anyway. Besides the public's acceptance of a ride, the ride's success depends on two other factors: capacity and repeat rides. The Loop-the-Loop failed on both. Since only one car, holding just four passengers, could complete the loop at a time, the ride couldn't take in

money at a fast enough rate to make back the heavy $400,000 investment. The Loop-the-Loop proved not to be a repeat ride as most of the riders took the loop, satisfied their curiosity, and went on to longer and more lasting thrills. Although a few Loop-the-Loops were installed in other cities in 1902, they were all financially unsuccessful and were all dismantled within ten years.

Yet despite the failure of its original Flip-Flap coaster, Sea Lion Park brought the customers in by the droves, who were now attracted to the idea of a single, enclosed amusement park. Right around the turn of the century, three more amusement parks appeared on Coney Island; three of the most lavish, spectacular, and sensational amusement parks ever built.

Chapter Three
Steeplechase Park, Luna Park and Dreamland

Looking east along Surf Avenue, c. 1890.
(Museum of the City of New York)

WHEN PEOPLE SAY "CONEY ISLAND," usually they are thinking of Steeplechase Park, by far the greatest and the best prototype of the old American amusement parks. A visit to Steeplechase meant a total escape from the world and its everyday cares and burdens. It was a place where man existed only in his folly and silliness, where the only sound which drowned out the bright melody of the carousel and the thrilling rumble of the roller coaster was the music of his own laughter, and where the phrase "It's a mad, mad, mad, mad world" never rang more true. The large sign which for decades pictured the huge, almost obscene grinning face (displaying no fewer than forty-four teeth) and read "Steeplechase: The Funny Place" was an understatement. It might have read "Steeplechase: Where good old American slapstick and humor was born and bred."

Steeplechase Park was the brainchild of the father and king of the American amusement park, one of the greatest showmen on Earth, George Cornelius Tilyou. Born in New York City in 1862, George grew up on Coney Island, surrounded by the wonder and attraction of the island's early visitors. His parents, Peter and Ellen Tilyou, were making a profitable living off their small hotel, the Surf House, which they had opened in 1865.

George must have had an extremely keen eye and ear for the desires of Coney's visitors as they gaily dropped into the Surf House and tasted his mother's famous chowder. He knew even than that people weren't coming to Coney looking for just a nice hotel and good food, nor were they Walt Whitmans who wanted to race up and down the lonely sand dunes. These people were looking for something new, different, and exciting, something that The Elephant or the Scenic Railway would later bring them.

Looking east along Surf Avenue, 1906. To the left of the Loop-the-Loop entrance at 10th Street is the Iron Tower, and to the right is the Dreamland Tower. (Brooklyn Public Library)

The Pike's Peak Railway was built by the L. A. Thompson Scenic Railway Company. (James A. Payer Collection)

George displayed his natural instinct as a Coney Island showman at the age of fourteen. That year, 1876, was the year of the Philadelphia Centennial Exposition, and Coney Island was full of people from the Midwest who had come east, not only to see the Exposition, but to take their first look at a real live ocean. George quickly set up a simple stand where he sold cigar boxes full of "authentic beach sand" and bottles full of "authentic salt water" for twenty-five cents each. The Midwesterners bought them faster than George could find the cigar boxes and empty medicine bottles.

When he was seventeen, George began dabbling in Coney Island real estate, taking advantage of the constant leases and subleases always going on. Many islanders were making a handsome living merely by leasing a lot and then subleasing fractions of it at a rate several times more than the original whole lot had cost. By working as a middleman, George began netting $250 a month.

As part of his real estate operation, George began publishing a four-page newspaper he called *Tilyou's Telephone.* Even here, his expertise as a showman came through. He knew of the supposedly therapeutic value of the seaside, and in advertising a cottage for rent he wrote that "convalescents from Typhoid Fever, those suffering from Malaria and Bronchial troubles, or those who desire and need rest from the cares and anxieties of their daily vocations can here derive a great benefit."

Besides real estate ads, George filled the paper with Coney Island news items, such as:

> It is said that the Brighton will introduce American fireworks the coming summer on their grounds.

> Feltman is getting his large Hotel and Dancing Pavilion in readiness for business, as he anticipates an early season.

George's famous Coney Island poem, "Sea Sonable," was presented in the *Telephone's* first issue.

> "Ocean me not," the lover cried,
> "I am your surf—to you I'm tied.
> Don't breaker heart, fair one, but wave
> Objections thine this sand I crave.

> "Oh billow Bill," she blushed. "I sea
> You would beach ozen shore by me.
> But I'm mermaid not yet in seine,
> And shell for years that way remain."

His poem pretty much sums up what Coney Island stood for: the sea, amusement, romance, and a little silliness.

However, it was not the real estate business that George was interested in, but show business. In 1882, when he was twenty, he and his father built Coney Island's first

George Tilyou in 1905,
in one of his rare unsmiling moments.
(Long Island Historical Society)

The trademark of Steeplechase Park, "The
Funny Place." (Courtesy Steeplechase Park)

45

The Bowery in 1912. (Brooklyn Public Library)

theater, the Surf Theater, where many of the soon-to-be-greats of vaudeville—Pat Rooney, Sam Bernard, and Weber and Fields—performed. George and his father wanted to make sure that the crowds of Coney would have no trouble finding the theater, so the two men cut an alley way that ran parallel to and directly between Surf Avenue (Coney's major thoroughfare) and the oceanfront, so that all of the walks which went from Surf Avenue to the ocean cut through it. They paved the alley with planks, and it was soon dubbed The Bowery, after the street on the lower east side of Manhattan. The Bowery became the famous promenade of Coney Island. As Coney grew, its rides, amusements, and sideshows grew around The Bowery, possibly the origin of the standard amusement "midway."

In 1893, George married New York girl Mary O'Donnell, and for their honeymoon they went to Chicago to see the World's Columbian Exposition, held in honor of the quadricentennial of Columbus's discovery of America. (The fair was to open in 1892, but the elaborate planning and construction caused a year's delay.) It was at this World's Fair that the actual "midway" was introduced, containing rides, shows, and concessions apart from the largely industrial balance of the fair. America's first two world's fairs, the New York Crystal Palace of 1853 and the Philadelphia Exposition of 1876, didn't have midways.

In visiting the Exposition, George was actually on the lookout for some new and inviting amusement he could bring back to Coney Island. He had had the same intention when he went to the Philadelphia Exposition in 1876, but once there he made the

The star of the 1893 World's Columbian Exposition: the original Ferris wheel. (Chicago Historical Society)

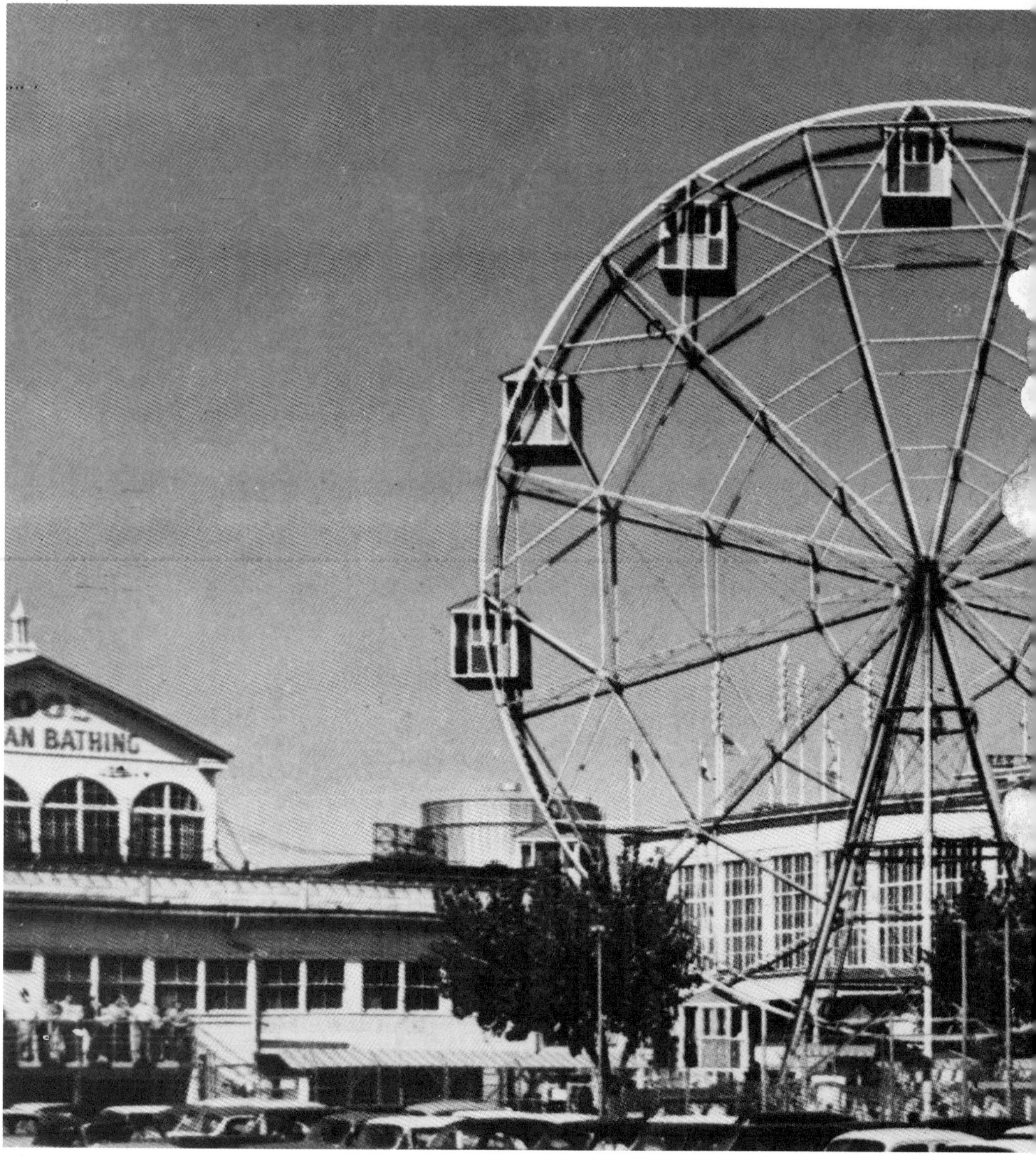
AN BATHING

George and Mary Tilyou's Ferris wheel is shown here at Steeplechase in the 1950s. While it wasn't a great money-maker in its later years, Mary Tilyou kept it out of sentiment for her late husband.

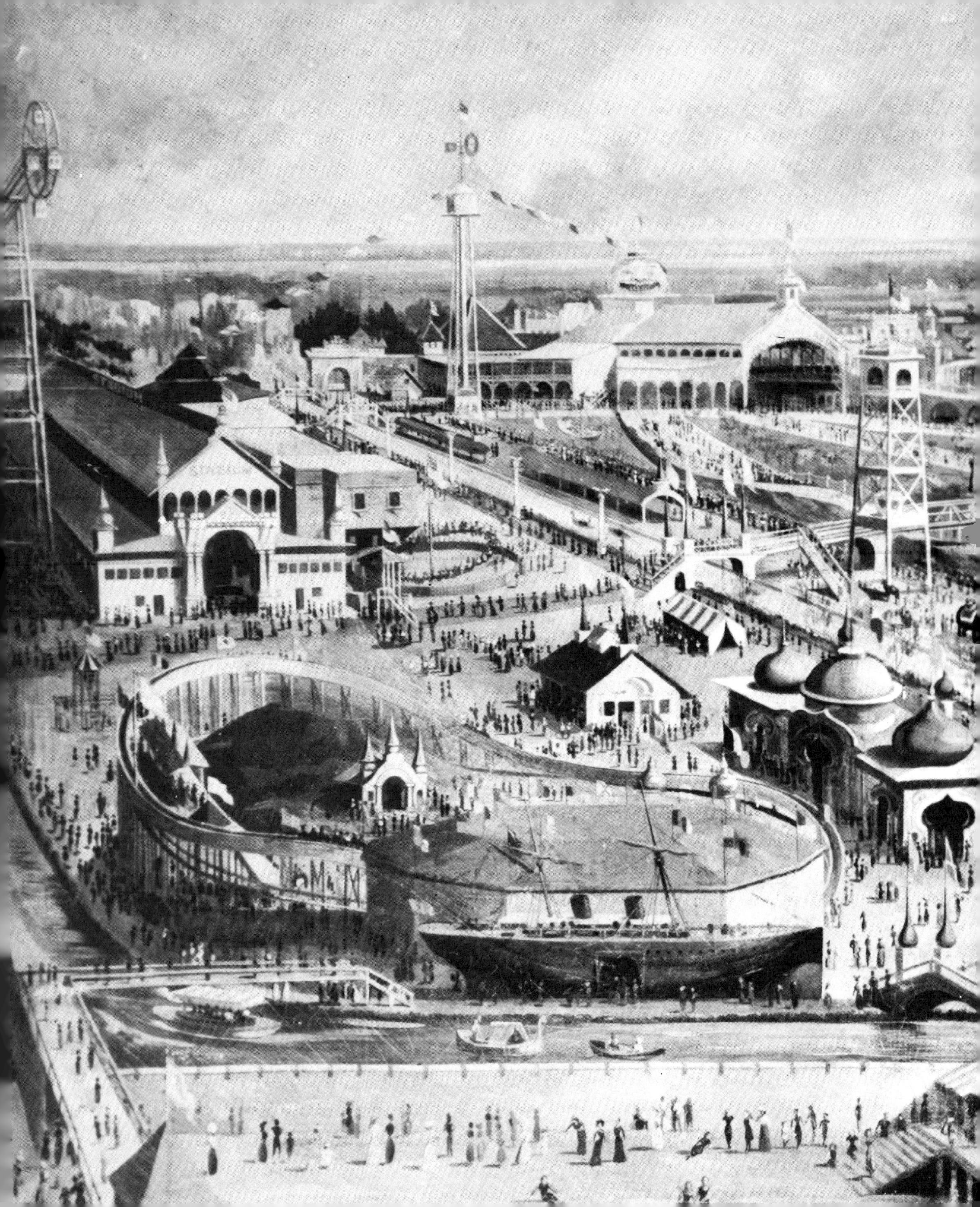
STADIUM

Steeplechase Park in 1903. Clockwise from the entrance at the bottom are the "Canals of Venice," a circular scenic railway, the "Giant Seesaw," an indoor cyclorama, the "Wedding Ring," an elephant ride, and the Steeplechase ride circuit. (Museum of the City of New York)

practical purchase of a horse which he took back to Coney. He constructed a simple stagecoach and began a brief but, as always with George, successful means of transportation from Coney's Norton boat landing on the west end of the island to the more active middle area, always urging his passengers to visit his parents' Surf House. At the end of the summer season, George owned six horses and two stagecoaches and, realizing his success, he sold them and began looking for something else to do.

What George and Mary Tilyou saw at the Chicago Exposition was a bit more astounding and unusual than a horse. They gazed upon the engineering feat of the year and the sensation of the Exposition, the giant Ferris wheel. It was designed and constructed by George W. Gale Ferris, a mechanical engineer from Galesburg, Illinois. He was involved in the planning of the fair, and at a conference prior to the fairground construction a delegate from France said that it was unfortunate that the Chicago Fair wouldn't have an architectural structure as impressive as that of the Eiffel Tower for the 1889 Paris World's Fair. Taking up the challenge, Ferris set to work designing what he felt would be the world's most thrilling and impressive structure.

Ferris wheels, called "pleasure wheels" before Ferris put his own name on them, had long been a popular amusement, ranging in height from 12 feet to perhaps 25 feet. They were wooden and run by manpower. George Ferris's steel wheel was mammoth almost beyond belief. It had a 250-foot diameter and held 36 cars, with 60 seats in each car. Completely full, the giant wheel held 2,160 people, who each paid fifty cents to enjoy the exciting trip into the sky. The news of the giant wheel spread all over the country, bringing people from the East and West coasts just to take a ride on the metal monstrosity.

After looking in amazement at the huge, slowly revolving wheel, Tilyou immediately sought out information for the purchase of the wheel. Alas, it had already been sold to the Louisiana Purchase Exhibition of 1904 in St. Louis. Undaunted, George decided to order a smaller Ferris wheel instead, 125 feet in diameter with 12 cars holding 18 passengers each. He and his wife then returned to Coney Island, where George leased a plot of land upon which he erected a sign that read without embarrassment: "On This Site Will Be Erected the World's Largest Ferris Wheel." The reaction to

The entrance to Luna Park, 1912. (Brooklyn Public Library)

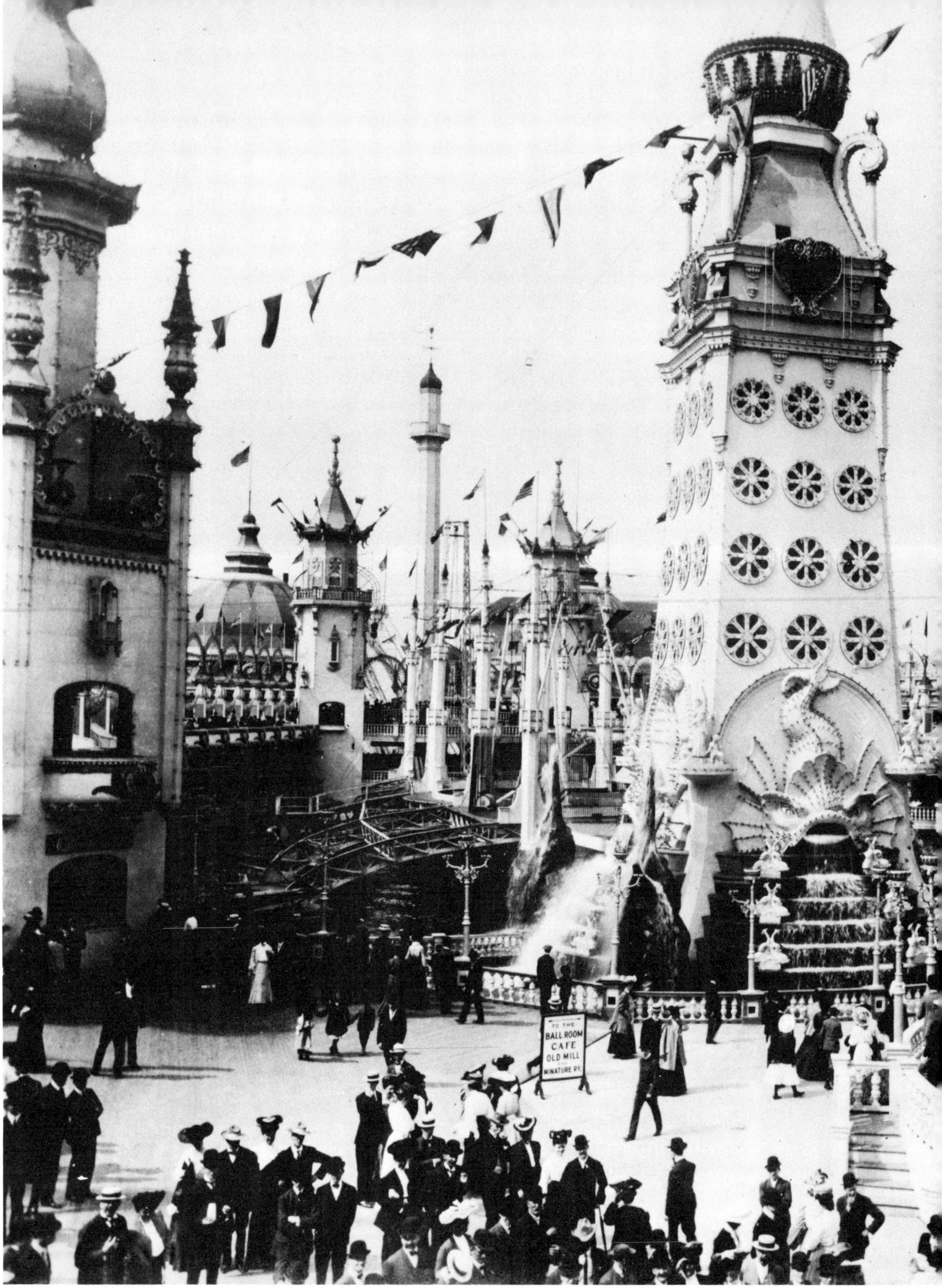
TO THE
BALL ROOM
CAFE
OLD MILL
AND
MINATURE RY.

Luna Park's tower and lagoon were just inside the entrance. c. 1905. (Museum of the City of New York)

*Sliding down the "Human Toboggan Slide"
in Luna Park, 1909. (Brooklyn Public
Library)*

Spires, minarets, towers, and lagoons were all part of Luna's attempt to awe the visitor. But it was fun they wanted. (Museum of the City of New York)

the sign alone enabled George to sell enough concession space around the wheel to pay for the wheel on delivery in the spring of 1894. He covered the wheel with hundreds of incandescent lights, and it immediately became the biggest attraction of Coney Island.

With the accent at Coney Island now leaning heavily toward amusements, George began surrounding his Ferris wheel with a few rides which included the standard carousel, a scenic railway, an aerial corkscrew slide, and a ride he imported called the Intramural Bicycle Railway. But George didn't get the idea of enclosing all of his attractions into one single amusement park until Sea Lion Park opened in 1895.

George was aware that Paul Boyton's Shoot-the-Chutes was the main ingredient that made Sea Lion Park a success, so he knew that he needed a new, enticing amusement that would pack in the customers to his newly planned amusement park. After some thinking, George realized that the most popular sport on Coney Island, horse racing, could also conceivably become the most popular amusement ride. When he learned of a recently British-invented mechanical racetrack, George knew he had hit the bull's-eye.

The Steeplechase Ride, as he called it, consisted of eight wooden double-saddled horses which coasted up and down an undulating curved metal track running from the starting gate to the finish line. It was as good an imitation of horseracing as one could get, and it was easily the stellar attraction of the 15-acre Steeplechase Park when it opened in the spring of 1897. George placed an admission price of twenty-five cents at the gate, and once inside, patrons could enjoy the various amusements as much as they cared to.

Steeplechase Park was an instant success, but George knew that constant addition and change would be necessary in order to keep the crowds coming. (The lack of Sea Lion Park's addition and change was the reason for its short popularity.) So, in 1901, he went on another amusement scouting trip, this time to the Pan-American Exposition at Buffalo. The attraction there that caught his eye, as well as everyone else's, was an illusion ride called "A Trip to the Moon," an exciting imaginary trip through space with a landing on the moon.

A Trip to the Moon was housed in a large round building in the center of which was a large raised spaceship with flapping wings. Thirty passengers would board the ship and peer out of portholes to the walls and floors of the room. After the captain's countdown, projections against the walls and floor gave the illusion of a blastoff from the fairgrounds, passing over Niagara Falls, and on up into space, away from a shrinking Earth, while the ship itself swayed and gave a feeling of motion. After passing through an electric storm in space, the spaceship would approach the moon and cruise over its prairies, canyons, and craters before making a landing. The passengers would then debark and pass through underground caverns and passageways inhabited by giants and midgets until they arrived at a grotto where the Man in the Moon sat on a throne, surrounded by dancing moon maidens. After a lunar welcome, the moon maidens escorted the group into a green room where they reminded them that the moon is made of green cheese, whereupon they would take bits of green cheese off the wall and offer them to the passengers. The passengers would then pass over a swaying bridge and emerge once again into the bright reality of the fair.

The rear of Luna Park, showing Hagenbeck's Wild Animal arena and Paul Boyton's old Shoot-the-Chutes, which was still the most popular ride in the park.
(Brooklyn Public Library)

Luna at night was a fairyland almost beyond belief. (Museum of the City of New York)

A Trip to the Moon was such a perfect visual, auditory and physical illusion that many people refused to believe that the ship had not left the room. This ingenious ride was owned by Frederic W. Thompson, an architectural student who had designed it one night when hunger kept him awake. Thompson formed a partnership with Elmer Dundy, and the two men made a small fortune at the Buffalo Exposition which assured them of no more hungry nights.

Tilyou approached Thompson and Dundy and offered them 60 percent of the net profits if they would bring A Trip to the Moon to Steeplechase Park. Since the two men would have no other place to display their amusement inventions until the St. Louis Exhibition of 1904, they readily agreed. Besides A Trip to the Moon, Thompson and Dundy took with them to Steeplechase two other creations, another illusion cyclorama, called Darkness and Dawn, and a ride called the Aerio Cycle (renamed the Giant See-Saw at Steeplechase), two small Ferris wheels on each end of a giant teeter, which would lift its passengers 235 feet into the sky, giving them a beautiful view of the fair and the city.

Wormword's Monkey Theater in Luna. (Brooklyn Public Library)

The Dragon's Gorge in Luna.
(Brooklyn Public Library)

Luna's most exciting show
was "Fire and Flames."
(Museum of the City of New
York)

Despite almost constant rain—always the fear and the gross-cutter in the outdoor amusement industry—during the 1902 season, Steeplechase was doing exceptionally well, due mainly to its new indoor cyclorama features. Business at Sea Lion Park, on the other hand, was down to almost nothing. Realizing their success with A Trip to the Moon, and hearing Paul Boyton's frantic cry to sell his Sea Lion Park before it folded, Thompson and Dundy decided to build their own amusement park, a park so spectacular it would, they believed, drive Steeplechase right into the Atlantic. Tilyou wasn't the least bit bothered by the duo's decision to start their own park; he knew that the more competition there was on Coney, the more the crowds would come, and more profits would be had by all.

So when the 1902 season and their pact with Tilyou was ended, Thompson and Dundy moved their Trip to the Moon east down Surf Avenue to Sea Lion Park, which they razed except for the Shoot-the-Chutes and the lagoon. On May 2, 1903, the two men threw open the doors of their $1,000,000 Luna Park, the second great Coney Island amusement park. Luna Park was a spectacular array of soaring minarets, spires, domes, ornate architecture, and monumental buildings, all covered with over 250,000 electric lights, presenting an almost blindingly colorful light show at night. In less than two hours after its opening, 40,000 people—at an admission of ten cents each—were walking wide-eyed through the 22-acre park.

Up and down Surf Avenue, Luna advertised its "Thirty-Nine Supreme, Stupendous, Spectacular, Sensational Shows! By day a Paradise—at night Arcadia!" Besides

The elephants' shoot-the-chutes in Luna. (Museum of the City of New York)

The 1930s saw a slightly altered Luna Park. (Ken Strickfaden Collection)

the top-billed showing of "A Trip to the Moon," Luna Park presented "A Trip to the North Pole," "The Dragon's Gorge," "Eskimo Village," "Monkey Theater," "Indian Village," "20,000 Leagues under the Sea," "Chinese Theater," "The Streets of Delhi," and "Hagenbeck's Wild Animals."

Luna Park also introduced several new ride sensations, one of the most popular of which was the "Mountain Torrent." This ride was a combination of a roller coaster and shoot-the-chutes. Passengers would ride up escalators or climb alpine paths to the top of an 80-foot mountain. There they would board tracked cars which raced down, around, and through the mountain in a flume carrying water at 35,000 gallons a minute, ending in a splash in a glacier lake at the bottom.

Another ride in Luna which, fortunately, never got past the experimental stage was the Leap-the-Gap coaster. It was a roller coaster whose car was drawn upward and into a large wooden cannon. After leaving the mouth of the cannon, it flew across a wide gap in the track, landing back on the track on the other side and completing its circuit back into the station. The ride was tried successfully several times with an empty car, but it didn't take the builders long to realize that any change in the car's weight due to passengers would change its trajectory, very likely resulting in a crash. The gap was therefore filled in, and the ride was opened up as merely the Cannon Coaster, which

Luna Park in the 1930s. (Ken Strickfaden Collection)

romantically advertised itself at its entrance with this ditty: "Will she throw her arms around your neck? Well, I guess, yes!"

Luna was the first amusement park to present the live spectacular show, theirs called "Fire and Flames." It consisted of the actual burning of a four-story building, complete with firemen and a rescue squad to save actual men and women trapped in the upper stories, who jumped to safety into the nets below.

In one of its advertising campaigns a few years after its opening, Luna Park announced for one week the public execution of an elephant. Topsy, one of the elephants in Luna's elephant act, was getting quite old and had to be given euthanasia. The method to be used was to feed her poisoned carrots, in an arena with a seating capacity for several thousand spectators who wanted to thrill to the elephant's death. But the thrill never came, and it was most likely the management's intention that the carrots were to have no effect on Topsy. Publicity stunts, they knew, should be milked for all they're worth in order to keep the crowds coming. So during the next week, Luna Park announced that Topsy would be electrocuted in the arena. Again, the weekend brought record crowds to Luna, as in between taking A Trip to the Moon and riding a scenic railway, they witnessed an elephant's electrocution.

Dreamland's entrance led past its top-billed attraction, "The Creation." (Brooklyn Public Library)

Despite such occasional vulgarities, Luna was, after all, grand, beautiful, exciting, and successful, and its success encouraged Thompson and Dundy to expand their enterprises to Manhattan, where they opened up the Hippodrome Theater on Sixth Avenue between 43rd and 44th Streets. The Hippodrome was gargantuan in every respect: it cost $3,500,000 and had seating for 5,200, making it the largest theater in New York City. Its sellout shows are still considered to have been the most lavish, spectacular, and expensive ever staged in the United States. One of the most popular acts in the shows was that of real elephants sliding down shoot-the-chutes. This act was later used in Luna Park as elephants slid down their own private shoot-the-chutes right alongside Paul Boyton's old Shoot-the-Chutes. In the 1930s, pigs began sliding down the chutes instead of elephants.

If the gross receipts of both the Hippodrome and Luna Park weren't proof enough of Thompson and Dundy's success, the opening of a third similar amusement park at Coney was. A year almost to the day after Luna's opening, Dreamland opened up on 15 acres of oceanfront property just across Surf Avenue from Luna. At a cost of $3,500,000 and employing a staff of 4,000, Dreamland seemed to close the book on the spectacular amusement park. Because it was patterned so closely after Luna, Dreamland was less

Dreamland's tower, supposedly a reproduction of the Tower of Seville, was the highest structure on Coney Island. (Brooklyn Public Library)

original, but it was certainly more lavish. Its magnificent 375-foot Beacon Tower gave off an illumination which could be seen several miles out at sea, the entire park was painted pure white and laced with massive and beautiful arches and columns; on a platform high above a large lagoon a band played continuously. On the acquired Iron Pier was a ballroom large enough for 25,000 dancers who danced to an orchestra playing under a giant seashell at the end of the pier. At night the entire park was lit by over 1,000,000 incandescent light bulbs, 100,000 of which picked the tower out against the night sky.

Dreamland had several of the rides and shows introduced in Luna, so many of them, in fact, that it seemed to be a reproduction of Luna, except on a much grander scale. It was owned not by showmen, but by several politicians who wanted to lend beauty and grandeur to the amusement park, rather than try for an original amusement park lure, like Boyton, Tilyou, Thompson, and Dundy had done. But although Dreamland could have been, and in fact was, accused of plagarism, it did have a few novelties, including "The Midget City," populated by 300 authentic Lilliputians, "Coasting through Switzerland," a scenic railway through a replica of the Matterhorn, "The Great Deep Rift Coal Mine of Pennsylvania," including a simulated cave-in, and

Everything Luna did, Dreamland topped. Its Shoot-the-Chutes was higher and had twice the capacity. (Museum of the City of New York)

the park's showstopper, called "Under and Over the Sea," a simulated airplane ride over the Atlantic and a submarine ride underneath it.

One of Dreamland's and the world's most unusual attractions was a ride called "The Haunted Swing." A dozen people would enter a square, furnished room in the middle of which hung a large 12-seat swing suspended from a beam stuck through the room. After the wary passengers were seated in the swing, some attendants would give the swing a shove and start it rocking forward and back. After the attendants left the room, the frightened passengers soon found that the swing was continuing to build momentum, arching higher and higher with each swing until it was making complete overhead loops around the room, again and again, gaining in speed, and then mercifully slowing, rocking again, and stopping.

The whole thing was, as usual, an illusion. The attendants, upon leaving the room, would actually set the entire box enclosure of the room into circulation, making it rock forward and back and eventually revolve around the swing, which had in reality stopped swinging after the few gentle rocks from the attendants' shove. The furniture

The Dreamland Bathing Pavilion, 1905.

and fixtures in the room were secured to the floor, walls, and ceiling of the revolving room. The illusion was so perfect that the passengers would grab onto each other in fright, even though they were informed of the trick before they entered, for safety's sake. The Haunted Swing was very successful for a couple of years, but as it wasn't a repeat ride, it stopped making money and was soon dismantled.

One of Dreamland's exhibits was called "The Infant Incubator," in which prematurely born babies were displayed in their incubators. The man in charge of this exhibit, Dr. Martin Couney, was able to save 7,500 out of 8,500 premature babies through his intensive research in childbirth. Highly respected by the American Medical Association, Dr. Couney ran his "sideshow" in a quiet and respectful manner, asking for silence from the spectators. He had many of the facilities of a modern hospital at hand, including several trained nurses. The money brought in by visitors to the Infant Incubator was enough for the operation to pay for itself, allowing mothers with premature babies to have them cared for without the expensive hospital cost.

Dreamland excelled on the popular "superspectacular," as it presented its grandiose biblical epic "Creation," and a $200,000 re-creation of "The Fall of Pompeii," with Mount Vesuvius erupting and killing 40,000 people, all of it simulated. Dreamland even topped Luna's "Fire and Flames" with its own "Fighting Flames," in which not a four-

By dawn of the great fire of 1911, Dreamland was only ashes and memories. The newly built "Giant Racer" was miraculously untouched by the blaze.

story but a six-story building was set afire amidst, again, fighting firemen, screams, and rescues.

This was Coney Island in its "Spectacular Era," when three great amusement parks presented every entertainment imaginable. As George Tilyou had said in *Tilyou's Telephone,* "If Paris is France, then Coney Island, between June and September, is the world." Everywhere was lights, color, music, action, and excitement, and what one park lacked, one of the others was sure to offer. Arrival at Coney Island by sea during the evening was a must, as in this way the glorious spectacle of a fantasy world was visible for almost a two-mile length of the island. It was this joyous sight—not the Statue of Liberty, as some suppose—that was the first glimpse of America that immigrants saw as their ships pulled into the New York harbor. They saw the part of America that laughed, sang, and was so incredibly alive.

In 1911, seven years after it opened, Dreamland outdid itself and presented what is known as the greatest Coney Island spectacle of them all: it burned completely to the ground. The fire started at two in the morning in an indoor dark ride ironically named "Hell Gate." Some workmen were preparing the ride for the next day's summer opening when some hot tar was accidentally ignited, quickly spreading fire throughout Dreamland. The inferno lasted until almost dawn, and while all the Dreamland employees escaped the blaze and the Infant Incubators were hurriedly removed, many of the wild animals burned to death. Some of the animals escaped from their cages, including one maddened and frightened lion who ran through the streets with a fiery mane, creating havoc and terror along Surf Avenue and The Bowery until he was shot at the top of a scenic railway.

The destruction of Dreamland was actually less sorrowful for the Coney Island frequenters than might be imagined. The park had been experiencing financial trouble in its seven-year history. While it was indeed bigger, cleaner, more beautiful, and had more rides and attractions than Luna or Steeplechase, it simply lacked the showmanship to pull in the crowds. People went into Dreamland and were awed by its grandeur and impressed with its array of amusements, but they went to Luna and Steeplechase and had fun. Luna and Steeplechase somehow had that laughter-charged atmosphere that Dreamland lacked.

After the fire came the Dreamland Circus Sideshow, and 1,000 freaks. (Museum of the City of New York)

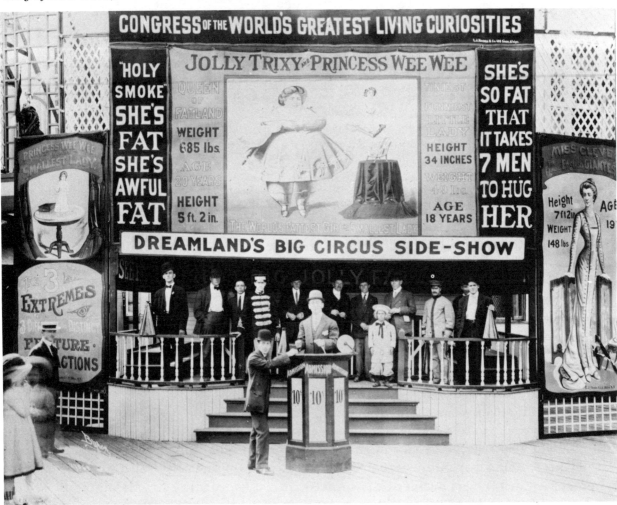

In a magazine article he wrote, Fred Thompson spoke of the talent he, Elmer Dundy, and George Tilyou had in stimulating amusement-park fun. "The difference between a theater and the big amusement parks is the difference between the Sunday school and the Sunday-school picnic," he wrote. "The picnic and the open-air park are designed to give the natural bubbling animal spirits of the human being full play. The first step, so far as the public is concerned, is to create an impression that there will be things doing, to get emotional excitement into the very air. When people go to a park or an exposition and admire the buildings, the exhibits and the lights without having laughed about half the time until their sides ached, you can be absolutely sure that the enterprise will fail."

Dreamland's last three years saw its owners frantically pouring money into the park to improve it, not quite understanding what it took to please the fun-loving Coney crowds. After the fire, one of the Dreamland businessmen said, "We sought to appeal to

While the freak became a mainstay on Coney after the Dreamland fire, the sideshow had been around since the beginning. This is the Original Turkish Harem in 1896, where gentlemen could have their wives "checked" while they watched the show, consisting mainly of belly dancers. (Museum of the City of New York)

Out of the over 300 midgets on Coney Island, the most famous was Mrs. Tom Thumb, shown here with Baron Magri and Count Magri, her second husband. (Museum of the City of New York)

a highly developed sense of the artistic, but it did not take us long to discover that Coney Island was scarcely the place for that sort of thing. Architectural and decorative beauty were virtually lost upon the great majority of visitors, with the result that from year to year Dreamland was popularized, that is to say, the original design abandoned."

Within hours after the Dreamland fire, Samuel Gumpertz, one of the park's managers (the man responsible for Lilliputia), set up what was to give him the title of the father of the sideshow and the freak. For several years Gumpertz had traveled extensively to Africa, Asia, and the South Sea Islands, searching for human mutations and aberrations. What he brought back to Dreamland was an impressive and frightening

Zip was the highest-paid freak on Coney Island. Despite his apparent abuse, he lived a happy eighty-four years.

This is the lady: the one and only Little Egypt.

array of freaks which were used in Dreamland's various shows and scenic rides, mostly as background and stage figures. After the fire, however, Gumpertz was able to display the freaks as he had always wanted—as a show in themselves. What he constructed on Dreamland's still smoldering ashes was the Dreamland Circus Sideshow, a presentation of African women who had stretched their lips up to 10 inches wide over wooden disks, Indian women who had lengthened their necks up to 14 inches by continually adding brass rings around their necks, and several "wild men" from various parts of the world.

Gumpertz continued to add to the Dreamland Circus Sideshow and to search the world for freaks, and within a twenty-five-year span he brought 3,800 freaks past the rather shocked faces of the U.S. customs inspectors. He also advertised for people to find new record-breaking freaks, offering for example $200 per inch for every inch above

Little Egypt's home was in the "Streets of Cairo," shown here in 1897. It became a part of Dreamland when the park opened in 1904. (Museum of the City of New York)

the world's tallest man, and $200 per inch for every inch below the world's shortest midget. Gumpertz's greatest desire was to find the fabled half man/half woman, but he never did. Evidently every man has his Seven Cities of Gold or Fountain of Youth.

The Dreamland Circus Sideshow took Coney Island by storm, and soon all up and down the Bowery there was the ballyhoo for this freak or that. There were fat ladies, tattooed ladies, bearded ladies, skeleton men, dwarfs, pinheads, strong men (Charles Atlas got his start on The Bowery), the Blue Man (who ate silver nitrate to make his skin blue), the Most Ugly Woman in the World (whose nervous disorder, called acromegaly, had thickened and distorted her bones, and, especially her face), the Monkey Girl (who had thick hair on her face and hands), and several pairs of Siamese twins.

The most popular freak on Coney was Zip, who was merely labeled a "what-is-it?" Zip was no more than a severely mentally retarded Negro boy who would jump up and down in his cage, screaming and flapping the arms of the dark, hairlike costume he wore. There is a story that Broadway producer David Belasco was convinced that Zip showed signs of intelligence, but he changed his mind when after throwing a fifty-cent piece into the cage, Zip picked it up and threw it right back at him.

Coney Island, the "Nickel Empire," in 1924,
showing the new boardwalk, the "Wonder
Wheel," and the "Giant Racer," which was
replaced by the "Cyclone" in 1928.
(Brooklyn Public Library)

If the hundreds of freaks who made their living at Coney Island were bothered by the gawking crowds, most of them learned to cope with their unhappy situation fairly well. But one of the more famous bearded ladies, Lady Olga, once said, "If the truth was known, we're all freaks together."

Of course, many of the freaks weren't really freaks at all, but merely tricky showmen. There was once a pair of beautiful Mexican Siamese twins who fell into a heated argument, and right in the middle of a show they separated and left the stage in a huff. The only person who was more shocked than the audience was the owner of the show, who had himself believed the girls to be authentic. He later said, "Those girls were tied together by a kind of corset. I guess I wasn't the first man to be fooled by a corset."

Although she wasn't part of the freak craze, easily the most famous of the Coney Island sideshow entertainers was torso-wiggling dancer Fahreda Mahzar, more commonly known as Little Egypt. Her first major appearance was at the World's Columbian Exposition in 1893, where she had created a sensation and was the only attraction to pull in more money than the giant Ferris wheel. She came to Coney in 1895 directly

For many years the Wonder Wheel was the highest Ferris wheel in America. It features cars which swing from the outer rim to an inner circle.

The Luna Park fire of 1946 was considered by most to be euthanasia. (Brooklyn Public Library)

after the fair's closing, and continued to play to standing-room-only crowds as she wriggled, shook, and slid-on-her-belly-like-a-reptile in the Streets of Cairo. Her several imitators also enjoyed her seven-year popularity until the Coney crowds, as usual, became bored and began looking for something different, at which time Little Egypt good-naturedly gave her last hootchy-kootchy, left the stage, and concentrated on being a wife and mother.

From the Dreamland fire on through the late 1920s, sideshow and freak-show owners enjoyed considerable success, whether they had fake or real freaks. But with the 1930s and the Depression, not only did they, like all other Coney operators, see an abrupt drop in the free-spending patrons, but they began finding it harder to collect authentic freaks. Modern medicine had found cures for the skin diseases and disfigur-

One of Coney's famous coasters, the "Mile Sky Chaser," was only kindling for the Luna fire. (Brooklyn Public Library)

Steeplechase Park's Pavilion of Fun in 1924, with the old Ferris wheel behind it and the Giant Seesaw to the right. (Brooklyn Public Library)

ing birth defects which created so many freaks. The increased medical knowledge of glands and hormones made it possible to treat various growth stunts or hormone imbalances. People with withered or no appendages could be fitted with artificial arms and legs. Siamese twins could be surgically separated. As freak-show owners therefore relied more on fake freaks, the public began losing interest in what they knew to be phony.

But the freaks craze of the 1910s and the resultant screaming barkers were only a prelude to what was to come in 1920: the Nickel Empire—when the New York subway system was extended to Coney Island, bringing New Yorkers only a nickel away from fun and the beach. The spires, minarets, towers, and showcases were gone, replaced by sideshows, barkers, hot dog stands, rides, and games, crooked or otherwise.

The Nickel Empire was an offensively loud and yet aesthetically exciting fusion of ballyhoo: "Come in and see Jolly Trixie, weighing in at 689 pounds; she's so fat it takes seven men to hug her!" "Ride the Wonder Wheel, the highest Ferris wheel in the

Steeplechase Park c. 1952, with the "Thunderbolt" roller coaster to the left and the "Parachute Jump" in the distance.

world! From its top you can see the Eiffel Tower in Paris!" "Guess your weight, guess your age, guess the make of your car—hell, I'll even guess your sex!"

The barkers' amplified screams were loud; the music blared; the shooting galleries rang; the coasters roared. Whereas during Coney's "Spectacular Era" the bright lights were visible to passengers out at sea, the noise of the Nickel Empire seemed to reach out even further. And whereas on a nice Sunday afternoon in 1900 there might be 100,000 Coney visitors, by 1925 the crowd would usually be over the 1,000,000 mark.

But this joyful pandemonium came to an end. In 1938, the beach and boardwalk came under the jurisdiction of the Parks Department, whose commissioner, Robert Moses, cracked down on the noise, telling the barkers to shut up or face arrest. The noise on The Bowery abruptly died down, and with it the customers temporarily did, too. Barkers were out of jobs, and the new Coney Island seemed dead. Even the gentle-voiced Dr. Couney of the Infant Incubators, relocated in Luna Park, was dismayed with the Parks Department's many new restrictions. "See all those rubbish cans lining the rail?" he said, pointing toward the boardwalk. "Moses put them there. Why, you used to come out here in the morning and find the boardwalk cluttered with all sorts of junk. Now look at it. It's clean. I have been here for thirty-five years, and I have known Coney Island when it was truly great. But the Island has gone backward, and now it has reached the end. Maybe Mr. Moses can restore it, but I don't know how. Maybe by force."

But the fears of a dying Coney Island were unfounded, as the 1940s seemed to automatically bring in large and constantly increasing crowds. The noise was lower, the prices were a little higher, the amusements were squeezed into a smaller area, but the fun and laughter mounted. It seemed that after all these years Coney's only real fear would be fire.

Fire was the ever-lurking menace to Coney Island and to all amusement parks. Because they are such an insecure investment, amusement parks up through the 1920s were made as cheaply as possible out of lath and staff. Lath is a thin wood, used in narrow strips to construct the framework of artificial mountains, false-front buildings, and the like. Staff is a composition of plaster of paris (named for its development at the Paris Exposition of 1878) and hemp fiber. This composition is molded into the desired shape and nailed into place against the framework. Such highly flammable material were responsible for amusement parks' exorbitant fire insurance rates. Both Luna and

Steeplechase Park's outdoor swimming pool, c. 1952.

Dreamland had to pay $5.50 per $100 of insurance they bought. Normal fire insurance rates at that time were $.03 per $100.

It was fire that eventually put an end to Luna Park in 1946, although the park had been having financial problems for many years, starting as early as 1907 with the death of Elmer Dundy. Going it alone, Thompson continued to manage Luna, but he was losing interest in the park and added few new rides or shows. Eventually the public turned away. But Thompson was becoming an alcoholic, and he died in 1919. The park was then taken over by a group of businessmen who, not being showmen, put very little money back into the park and let Luna slide and crumble. Two major renovations in 1935 and 1941 by two new sets of owners failed to bring the public back, and after the fire of 1946, the once fabulous Luna Park became a parking lot. A charred, skeletal end of the Mile Sky Chaser roller coaster stood for a few years at the side of the parking lot, a hearttugging reminder of the Spectacular Era of Coney Island long gone.

Fire had also dealt what had looked like a fatal blow to Steeplechase back in 1907, when the entire park was burnt almost to ground level. George Tilyou, surveying the damage at sunrise, allowed himself one second, maybe two, to feel sorry for himself. Then he immediately ordered his workmen to construct a fence around the ashes with an entrance and a sign that read:

Inside the Pavilion of Fun in 1910. The gaiety and laughter were infectious. (Brooklyn Public Library)

I had troubles yesterday that I have not today.
I have troubles today that I had not yesterday.
On this site will be erected a bigger, better Steeplechase Park.
Admission to the Burning Ruins—10 cents.

First, last, and always, George Tilyou was a showman.

Tilyou saw the fire as a benefit; in building a new park, he could avoid the mistakes and inadequacies of his old park, and he could put to use his own theory on what makes a successful amusement park. Tilyou felt that people will pay any price in order to provide their own entertainment. Whereas Dreamland tried to amaze and astound its visitors, Tilyou let the visitor himself get up on the stage and laugh at himself and his fellow man. He therefore built his new Steeplechase Park to allow its visitors be the main show.

Construction began immediately after the fire. The usual outdoor rides and at-

The "Human Roulette Wheel" was still popular in 1939, and still offered a view of ankle. (Museum of the City of New York)

tractions went up, along with a large outdoor swimming pool, and of course, a new Steeplechase ride. Within the Steeplechase Ride circuit, the 5-acre Pavilion of Fun went up, and it was here that George Tilyou's theory was put into long-lived success.

The Pavilion of Fun became the center for American humor, with the addition of exhibitionism and light sex. George knew that the outdoor amusement park was one of the few places, at least in his time, where a public embrace was acceptable, or where a flashy show of ankle from under a floor-length dress would not be considered lewd or suggestive. After all, who could blame a young woman for throwing her arms around her escort in fright as a roller coaster made an earthbound plunge, and how could that same girl keep her dress completely down while sliding down a wildly twisting slide? Dashingly brave young men and helplessly screaming young women were all part of the Steeplechase fun.

Admission to Steeplechase Park was fifty cents, which included all of the rides

Artist Reginald Marsh made this somewhat biblical rendering of the Pavilion of Fun in 1944. In the foreground is the "Dew-Drop" and the "Human Pool Table." (Museum of the City of New York)

As the Human Whirlpool spinning disc gathered speed, it flung its cargo from the center off onto the hardwood floor. The more crowded it was, the more fun. 1939. (Brooklyn Public Library).

and attractions. Upon entering the Pavilion of Fun, a couple could rent clown suits in order to protect their city clothes, and from there on it was madcap adventure. The couple would enter the "Barrel of Love," a revolving barrel lying on its side which jostled and slid its human cargo along its smooth interior mercilessly until the couple emerged dizzy-eyed from the other side. The placement of the Barrel of Love at the entrance of the Pavilion of Fun had a reason: those who entered it alone more often than not emerged with a date for the evening.

From there on, the wild fun was everywhere. One contraption was called, in the romantic fashion of Coney, the "Wedding Ring." It was a simple circular beam held three feet above the floor by cables. After fun-seekers would sit insecurely on the wooden beam, a few strong men would rock the beam to and fro, providing the women with a chance to clutch their men, as well as give a classy show of ankle.

Another of Tilyou's inventions was the "Human Roulette Wheel," which is fairly self-descriptive. Several people would sit in a concave bowl that would begin spinning slowly, picking up speed and tossing out some of its passengers, and mixing the rest up in a swirl of stomach-grabbing laughter. This was one roulette game where everyone won.

And they're off—around the Pavilion of Fun along the 1,400-foot track.

The start of the famous Steeplechase Ride, 1939. After the fire of 1907, the eight wooden horses

became four metal ones. A new race was started every thirty seconds. (Brooklyn Public Library)

At the end of the Steeplechase Ride, the only way out was across the "Insanitarium" in the Pavilion of Fun, 1939. (Brooklyn Public Library)

51.

Probably Tilyou's most ingenious invention was the "Human Pool Table." It was set strategically at the bottom of the "Dew Drop," a 50-foot circular slide. A woman hitting the bottom of the Dew Drop would land on a flat spinning disc, one of sixteen spinning discs laid into the metal "pool table" floor. She would quickly be flung to a second spinning disc, and to a third, and on to a fourth.

Outside the Pavilion of Fun, the grand Steeplechase Ride continued to pack in the customers, as they mounted their metal horses and made a dashing lap around the track, each determined to win first place. (The horse with the most weight always won, and it was not uncommon to find hefty and unescorted girls standing around the entrance to the ride, hoping some "jockey" would take her on his horse.) After the horses would reach the finish line, the riding couple would dismount and walk down one of two narrow corridors. Both corridors led to a brightly lit stage called the "Insanitarium," where the couple would be conscious of the anticipated laughter of a crowd somewhere beyond the bright lights. Suddenly, a strong burst of air would shoot up from the floor, lifting the woman's dress a few inches and giving her a chance to cry in distress. When the man would try to help her, a sprightly little clown would touch him with an electric wand, giving him a mild shock. The two would then race across the stage, straight for a high stack of barrels that would begin to shake and bend as if to topple upon them. The frightened couple would hesitate, but another shock from the clown would send them off the stage and out into the massive crowds of the Pavilion of Fun. If they cared, the embarrassed and self-conscious young man and woman could take a seat in the bleachers facing the stage, where they would soon be sent into gales of laughter watching others go through the same light, humorous torment.

So did Steeplechase Park affect everyone who entered it with unrestrained, raucous, stimulating, and just plain wild fun and laughter. Unfortunately, George Tilyou saw his glorious park only in its first seven years of operation. He died in 1914, and his eighteen-year-old son Edward took over the park's management, aided by his two brothers and two sisters. George's wife Mary survived him until 1954.

Steeplechase Park has survived over a dozen Coney Island fires, two world wars, and a Depression, and yet it has not lost its popularity. Today, millions of New Yorkers still storm Steeplechase on a summer weekend. But the park exists more in its past than present, as several changes have altered the Steeplechase character. In 1966, the Pavilion of Fun was regrettably torn down. Not only was the building getting old, but the Coney crowds had begun spending more time outside, and gradually the noise and fun in the pavilion died down. That same year, the Steeplechase Ride was dismantled and removed to Pirates' World, a fairly new amusement park at Dania, Florida, north of Miami.

The amusement section of Coney Island is now sixteen blocks long by two blocks wide, just a fraction of what it was at the turn of the century, when a two-mile stretch of island was full of amusements. But for all its changes and losses, the "Coney Island Experience" is still to be had. From the first step out of the subway station located at Surf and Stillwell Avenues you are greeted with a red and white sign that screams "Welcome to Coney Island!" and you're then bombarded with the sights, sounds, and

Dropping down the Parachute Jump to a summertime Coney beach and boardwalk in the 1940s.
(Brooklyn Public Library)

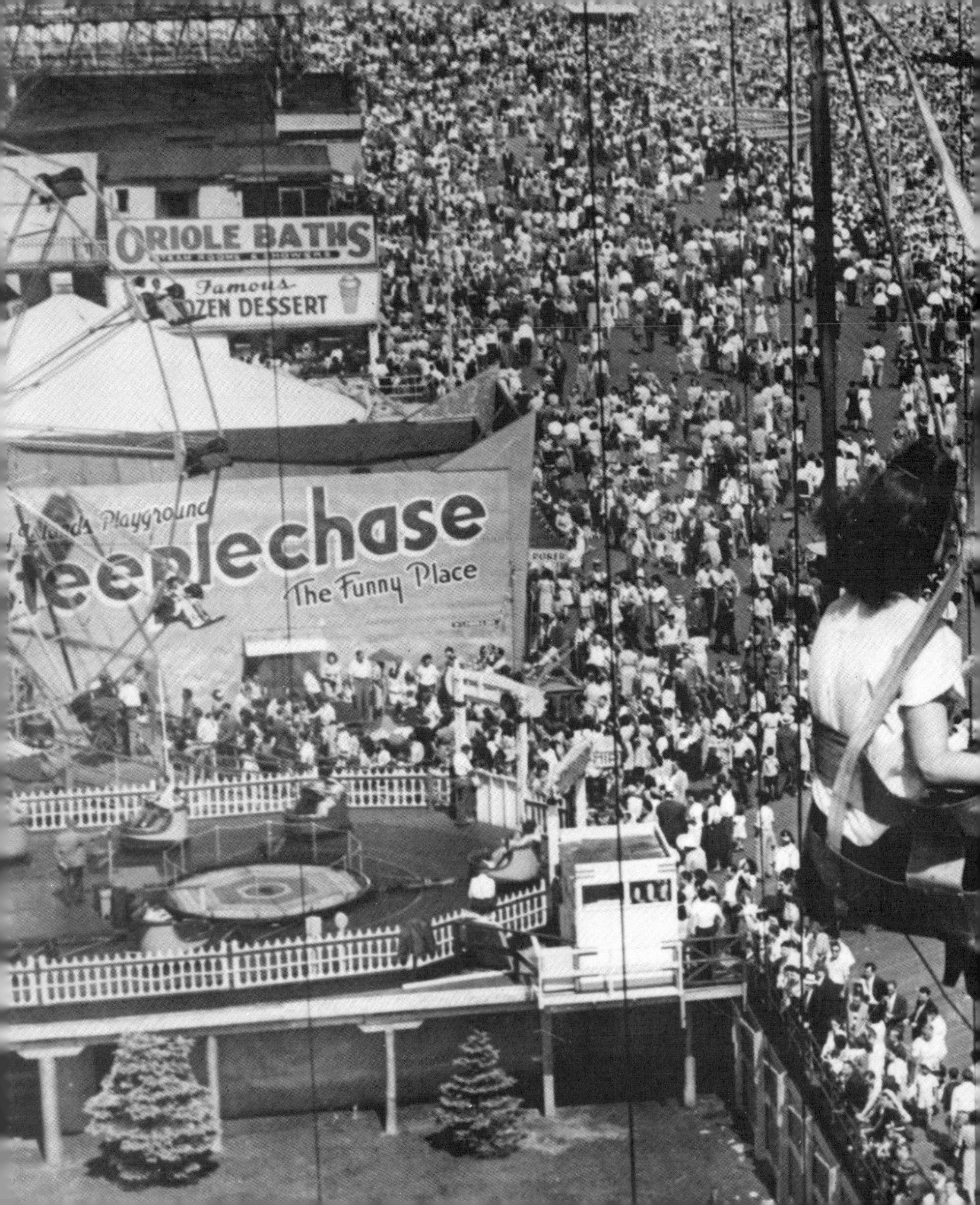
ORIOLE BATHS
Famous
ZEN DESSERT
Playground
eeplechase
The Funny Place
POKER

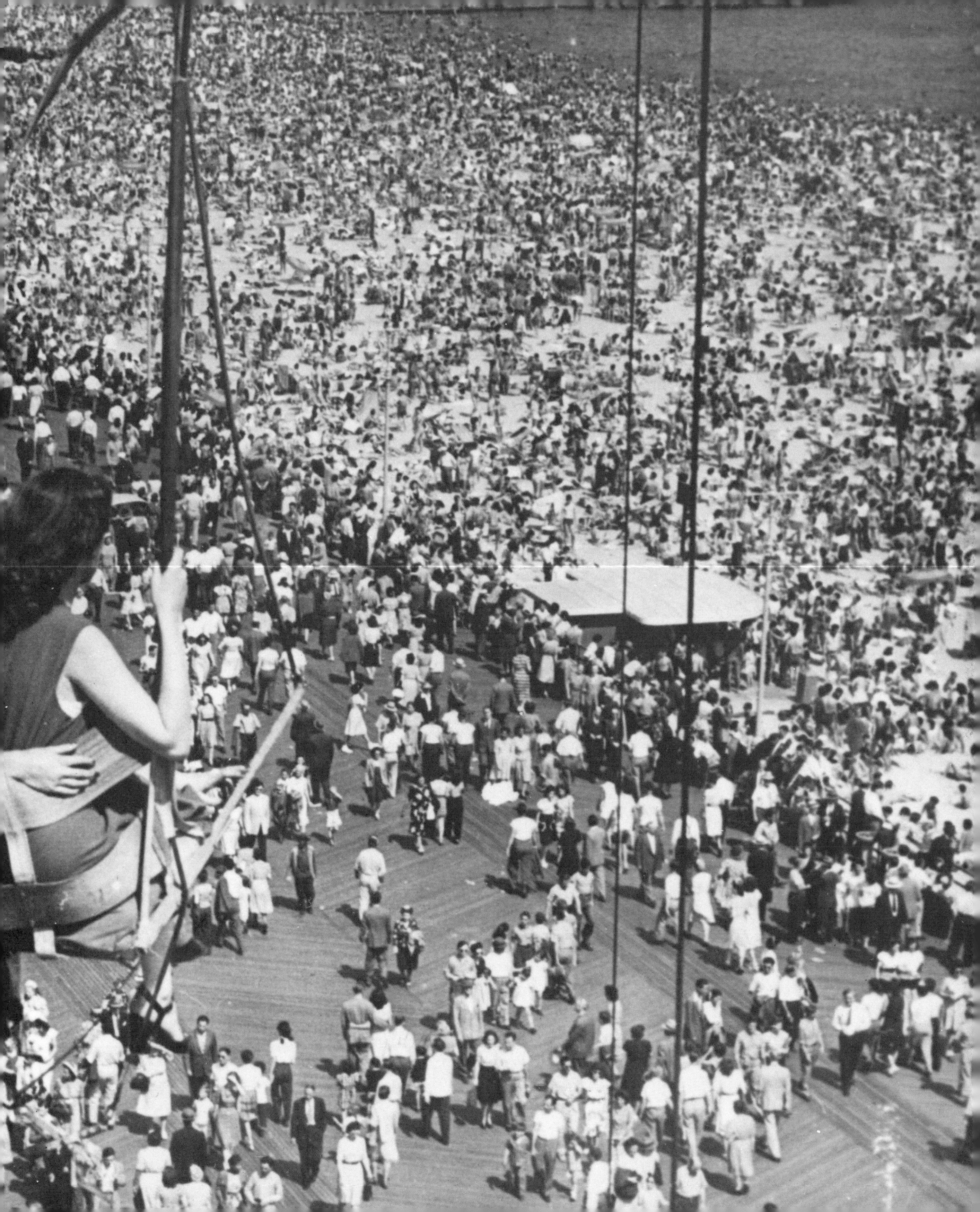

The Bowery today: a little the worse for wear, but hanging in there.

smells which take you out of yourself and into a world where people smile and enjoy themselves, and where care and worry are things forgotten. Nathan's Famous is still serving the best hot dogs in the world, the Cyclone is still the best roller coaster in the world, and the laughter still reigns supreme.

One other enclosed and singly owned amusement park at Coney besides Steeple-chase Park is Astroland, a half block worth of new amusements on the corner of Surf Avenue and West 10th, across the street from the Cyclone. All of the rides, games, and attractions between Steeplechase on West 26th and Astroland on West 10th are each privately owned. These include eight Dodgems, seven dark rides, five roller coasters,

The Thunderbolt coaster makes its initial dive.

three Ferris wheels, four go-carts, three fun houses, four kiddielands, and three carousels.

While a battle has been going on for several years between those who want the amusements torn down for high-rise apartments—which had already begun crowding the island after the 1935 fire—and those who want them preserved, it looks like the old Coney Island will be, for a time anyway, unsinkable. While it is true that New York's focus on Coney Island is now the beach rather than the amusements, if the amusements are removed, it will be the final sad erasure of one of the greatest American legends.

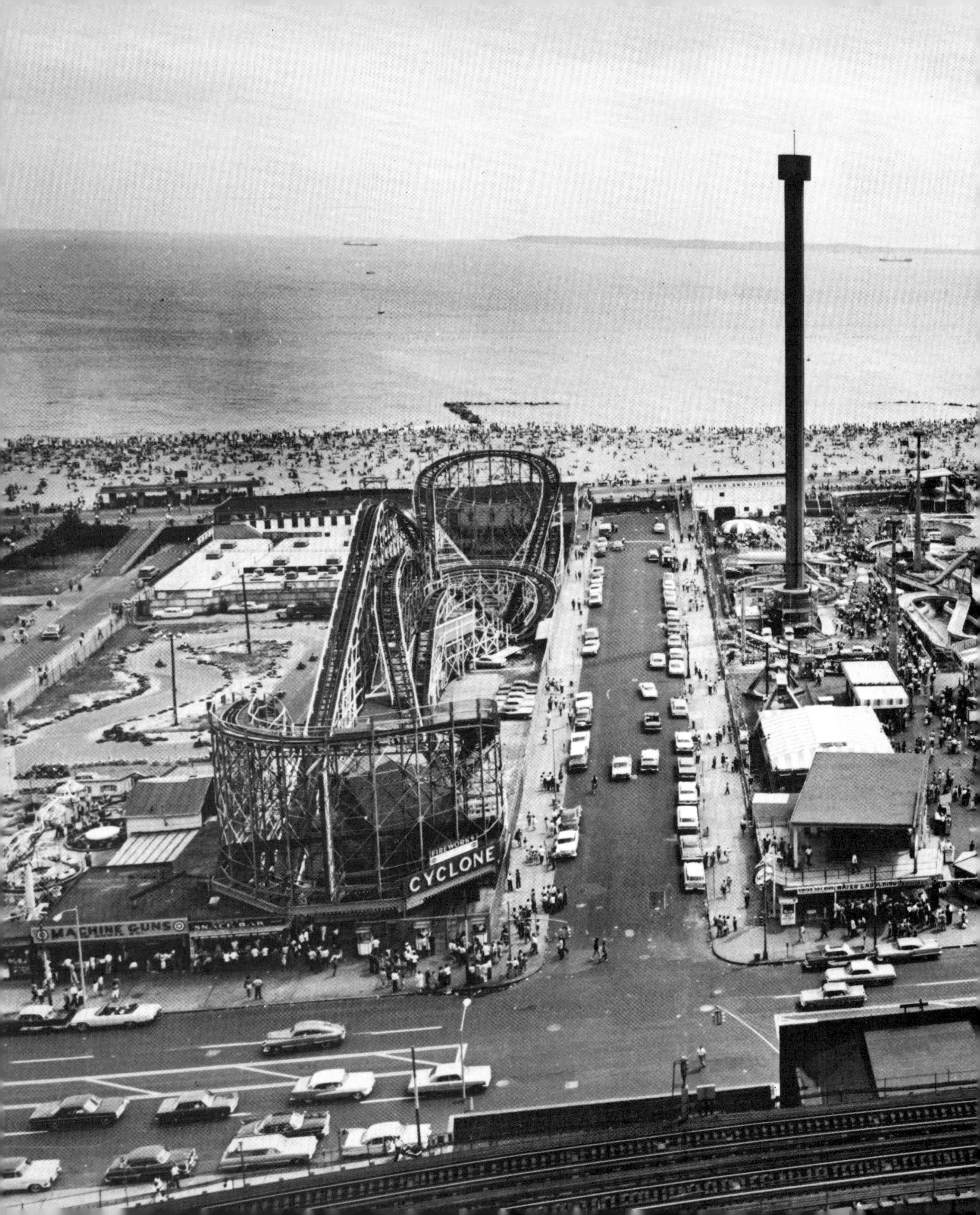
FIREWORKS
CYCLONE
MACHINE GUNS

This is Coney Island in 1964, basically the same as it is today. The area to the left of the Cyclone was once Dreamland and is now occupied by the New York Aquarium. To the right of the Cyclone is Astroland. Just past Astroland is the Wonder Wheel and the individually owned amusements. The Steeplechase Pier is in the right distance, and to the far right Steeplechase Park begins. The playground this side of the subway tracks was once Luna Park.

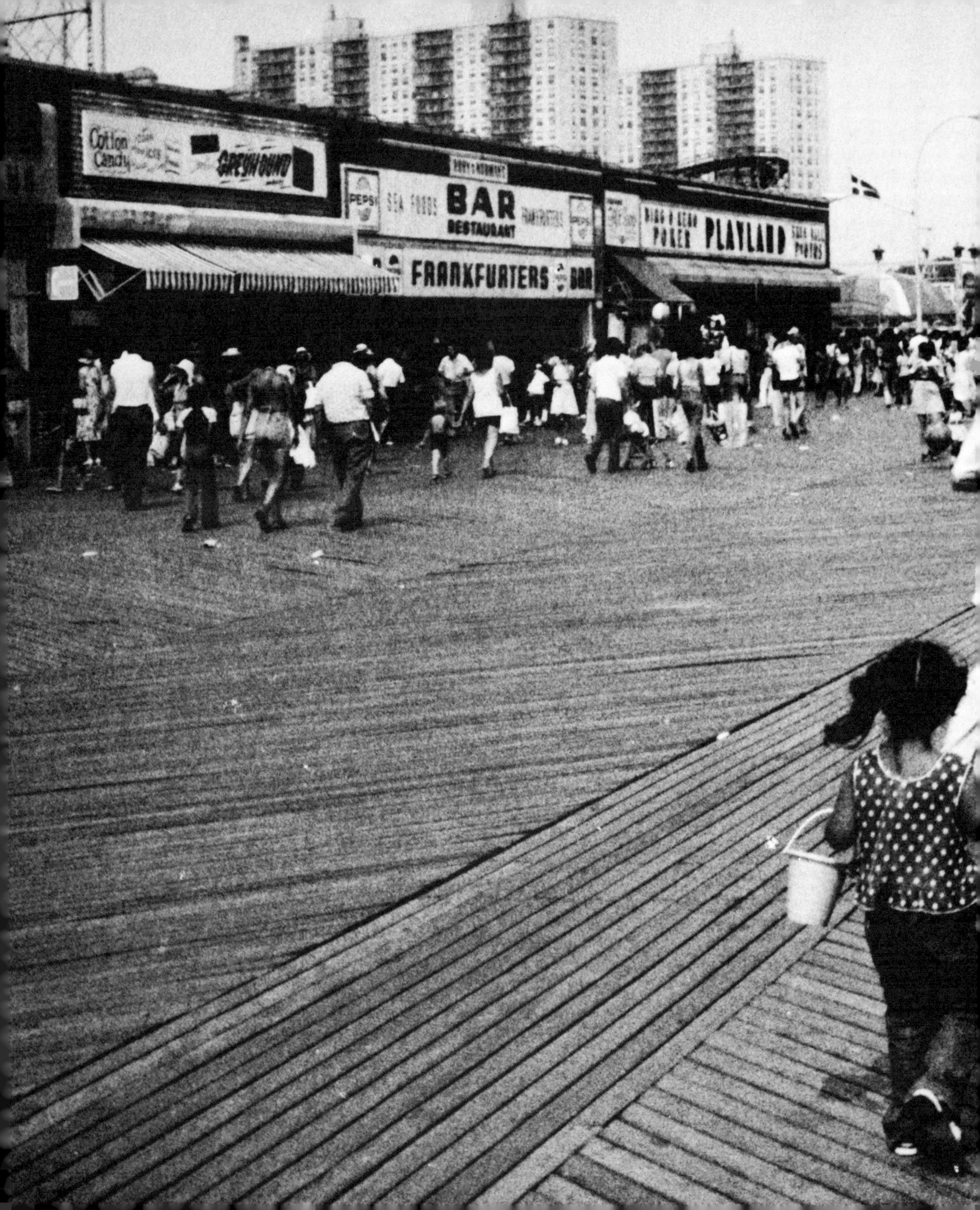
Cotton Candy
PEPSI
SEA FOODS
BAR
RESTAURANT
FRANKFURTERS
BAR
POKER
PLAYLAND

There has been over half a century of strolling the Coney Island boardwalk.

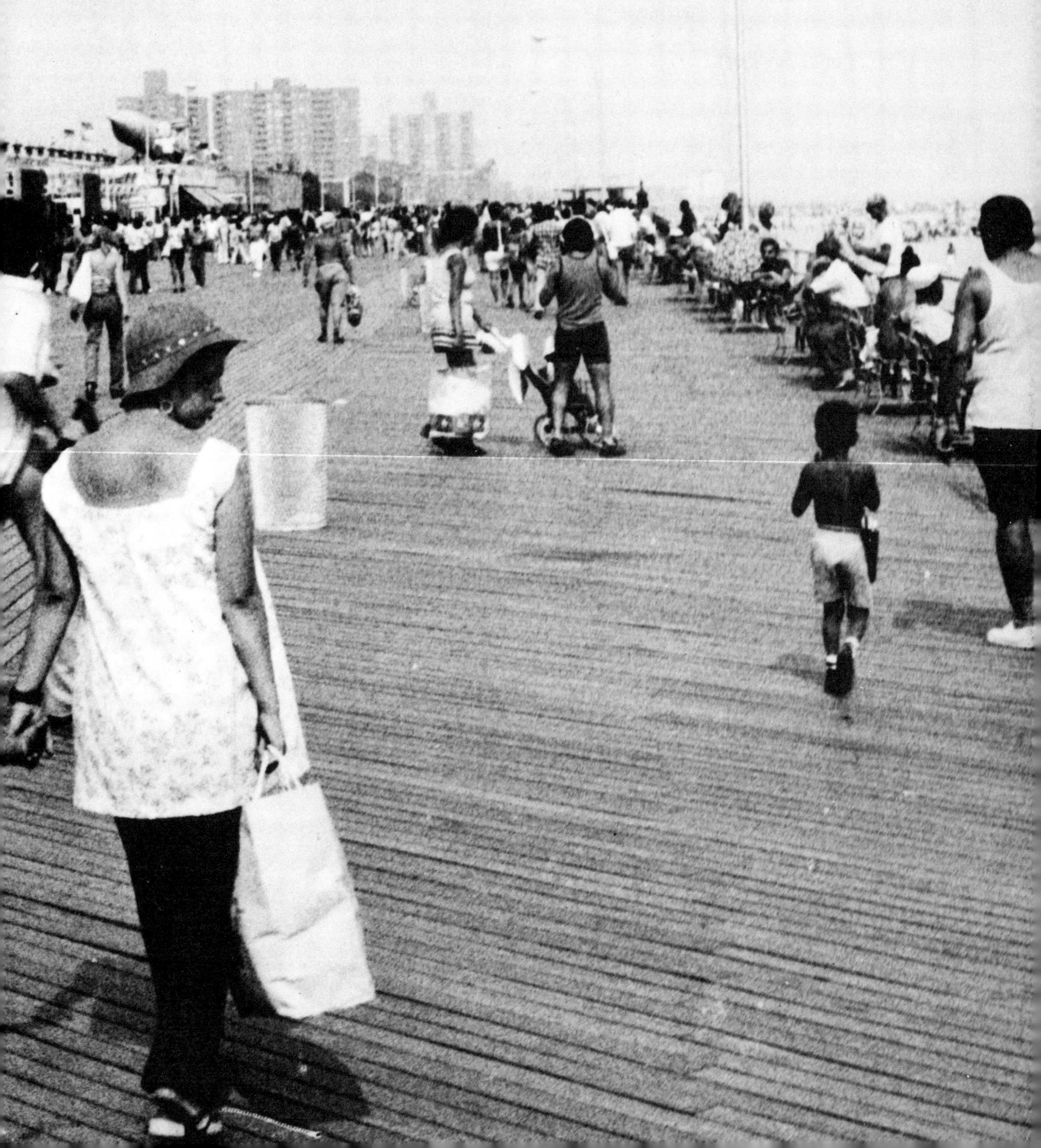

Chapter Four

The American Amusement Parks- East to West

THE SUCCESS of Coney Island and its amusement parks at the turn of the century led to an astonishing growth of amusement parks throughout the United States. By 1919, there were over 1,500 amusement parks in the country. Every city of decent size had a park, while the major cities had anywhere from two to six parks. It was almost possible to ride from the East Coast to the West Coast on roller coasters.

The American public was caught up in the outdoor amusement craze, and on almost every warm summer afternoon and evening you could find the typical American family at the local amusement park. With such a huge market, neighboring amusement parks had no trouble sharing the surrounding populations and pulling in large grosses. At the beginning

Kennywood Park, located just south of Pittsburgh, was one of the hundreds of trolley parks which sprung up near the beginning of the century. This photo was taken during the park's opening year in 1899.

This is Ulmer Park c. 1920, when it was one of the several amusement areas that lined Brooklyn's oceanfront. (Ken Strickfaden Collection)

Ulmer Park in Brooklyn was a typical trolley park, as shown by this old ad. (Brooklyn Public Library)

Idora Park at Youngstown, Ohio, was a trolley park which, like Kennywood, is immensely successful to this day. It is shown here in the 1920s.

of the 1920s and the Jazz Age and Prohibition, the public began to thirst even more for the type of thrills and excitement only an amusement park could provide for the average person. Charles Lindbergh made his heroic flight across the Atlantic Ocean and park customers began flying at breathtaking speeds on circular airplane rides. The daredevil antics of automobile stunt drivers made people delight in the seemingly reckless speed of the roller coaster. Everything was fast, thrilling, exciting, and no one was satisfied unless they felt their breath forced out of them or their stomachs dropping eight stories. Engineers and designers in the new industry of amusement rides racked their brains trying to find newer and yet safe ways to frighten and thrill park customers, who loved

to pay money in order to be scared out of their senses.

Most of the amusement parks at this time were known as "trolley parks." These were built by transit companies who wanted an incentive for people to ride their lines. Trolley parks were constructed at the end of the trolley line, almost always on some large body of water, and several miles outside of the city. On weekends and summer mornings people would crowd the small, open trolley cars and ride out for a day of amusements, picnicking, bathing, and relaxation. At the end of the day, the little cars would carry the tired and happy crowds back to the city.

The parks of the 1910s and 1920s were basically rides and games parks, unlike the spectacular shows and illusions

"Cyclone Bowls" Speed Thrill Seekers Up and Down Precipitous Whirlpools of Delirious Motion while Others May Enjoy an Orgy of Dish-Breaking

The November 1924 issue of Popular Mechanics *featured an article on the rides and games of Coney Island's Nickel Empire. Shown here are the unsuccessful "Cyclone Bowls" ride and a rather unusual "game." (Courtesy* Popular Mechanics*)*

World War II brought about a patriotic theme to the games in America's amusement parks. On Coney Island, the "Mow-'Em-Down" game consisted of shooting pellet guns at German paratroopers. This game was invented by Charles Feltman, the grandson of Mr. Hot Dog himself. (Brooklyn Public Library)

that dominated Coney Island's Luna and Dreamland parks. While Coney Island's Spectacular Era was ended with the Dreamland fire, the live spectacle would have come to an end shortly afterward anyway. Newsreels and motion pictures took the place of a simulated sinking of the *Titanic* or the Galveston Flood. So the American amusement parks concentrated on giving the customer thrilling rides and spacious picnic areas.

Also taking the place of spectacular shows were games and penny arcades, which began coming into their own in the 1910s. The first games, and the ones with the earliest origin, were the shooting galleries. This skill game grew out of target shooting, which dates back to the days of the bow and arrow. Outdoor target shooting became very popular in the European pleasure gardens and American picnic groves, and soon enclosed shooting galleries with stationary targets began to appear. After the turn of the century, shooting gallery operators installed movable targets, with jumping fish, flying ducks, rabbits, and bears parading across the target area.

Other skill games that became popular in amusement parks were dart-throws at balloons, ring toss, and baseball throwing at anything you could imagine, including live human beings. In amusement parks in the East during the

Skee ball is a skill game that is still popular. Redeemable tickets are awarded according to points scored.

Steeplechase Pier in Atlantic City, seen here in 1903, was in no way connected with George Tilyou's Steeplechase Park. At that time it presented live bands, as it here advertises for John Philip Sousa. Today, Steeplechase Pier is an amusement pier. (James A. Payer Collection)

Young's Pier in Atlantic City had a Loop-the-Loop. Steeplechase Pier is visible through the center of the loop. (James A. Payer Collection)

In 1906 Asbury Park was another popular New Jersey seaside amusement resort, and it still is today. (James A. Payer Collection)

Parker's Grove in the early 1880s.

The circular airplane ride, first presented in Luna Park in 1904, was very popular in Cincinnati's Coney Island. (Cincinnati Historical Society)

1910s and 1920s, there was a game called the "African Dodger," where patrons could throw three baseballs for ten cents at the head of a living Negro stuck through a canvas backdrop. The man could quickly dodge his head up and down or from side to side to avoid the balls, but that didn't always protect him from obtaining several serious blows on the face and head from a skilled baseball thrower. When the African Dodger was eventually banned by the Supreme Court, the concessionaires put in blackface dummies in order to continue to prey upon the racism of some park patrons. Fortunately such games are all in the past.

The prizes for skill games were usually not worth the money contestants

The come-on was usually better than the actual shows, but this never stopped crowds from pouring in, as they did at Cincinnati's Coney Island. (Cincinnati Historical Society)

The Island Queen 2 was one of the many steamboats that transported the Cincinnati population to Cincinnati's Coney Island. This 1931 crowd is debarking for a day of fun at Coney Island.

Cincinnati's Coney Island during the disastrous flood of 1937. (Cincinnati Historical Society)

This is the mall just before Cincinnati's Coney Island closed in 1971. The park's successor, Kings Island, re-created this area in one of its sections.

After the flood, Cincinnati's Coney Island continued stronger than before, as is shown here on the mall in the mid-1940s.

would spend, being either cheap wooden canes, hats, candy, or little plaster dolls called Kewpie dolls, the long-lived darling of prizes in the American amusement parks. Winning a Kewpie doll for a girl usually meant she was yours for the night—or for life. During the Depression, however, prizes for skill games became more practical, such as coffee, sugar, or crackers. People did not have the money to spend on a game that *might* yield them a wooden cane or a whistle.

The most successful skill games were ones that combined gambling with exhibitionism, and by far the most popular of these were the weight guessers. The usual routine would be for someone to stand up on the platform while the barker would touch various parts of the body with his pointer, giving him a good idea of the mass of the contestant. If the contestant was female, the routine would be all the more entertaining for the gathered crowd, and the barker's wisecracks would be all the more suggestive.

But any experienced weight guesser has no need for the pointer, and they used them for more than just a titillating

This "Most Beautiful Grandmother Contest" was held at Steeplechase Park. The competition between Steeplechase and Palisades Park for such gimmicks went on for years. (Brooklyn Public Library)

Easton's Beach, located in Newport, Rhode Island, is seen here c. 1920. (James A. Payer Collection)

show. As it often happened, the guesser could discover where a contestant was keeping his wallet, and by signaling to his accomplice in the crowd, he could let him know where to pick the man's wallet from once he stepped down from the platform. Some crooked weight guessers reported making as much as $7,000 in one season from this practice.

Penny arcades also became amusement-park mainstays by the 1910s, although coin-operated entertainment machines had been around for some time. In the 1880s, the Sea Beach Palace on Coney Island had boasted penny-operated machines which would set locomotives and steamships into sound and motion. By 1910, amusement-park patrons could, for the insertion of a penny, drive slot cars, find out their fortunes, watch historical events, take a scenic tour, or have their strength of grip tested. Couples could have the emotion of their kiss measured, and men could look at what at that time were considered rather erotic shots of young women clad in bathing suits.

Almost every amusement park had a penny arcade, although the penny of the 1910s and 1920s became the nickel and dime of the 1940s. Today, arcade games usually consist of computer-style games, costing a quarter to operate. They range from elaborate simulated war games to outer space flights to electronic table tennis. Then there are the always popular pinball machines, with steel balls that bump and roll their way around a maze of "100 Points When Lit" score targets.

One of the earliest of the American amusement parks was Parker's Grove, located on the banks of the Ohio River about twenty miles from Cincinnati. It was an apple orchard until about 1850,

Chicago's Riverview Park during the 1905 construction, showing the Shoot-the-Chutes, carousel, and roller coaster.

when it was converted into a picnic grove, giving the residents of the Ohio River valley the usual assorted amusements of picnicking, refreshments, target shooting, dancing, and a mule-operated carousel. In 1886, in the wake of Coney Island's amusement ride craze, Parker's Grove was taken under new management and opened up as an amusement park called "Ohio Grove, the Coney Island of the West." Within a few months, just the name "Coney Island" stuck.

Cincinnati's Coney Island grew into one of the nation's largest and most successful amusement parks by the turn of the century. At that time its biggest attraction was a novelty called the automobile. For a nickel, people took their first ride in a horseless carriage around a short oval course.

Riverview Park in 1915, when the dips were gentle. (Chicago Historical Society)

Miniature trains first became popular at the Philadelphia Centennial Exposition of 1876. Shown here is the miniature railway at Riverview Park in 1916. (Chicago Historical Society)

The major reason for Coney Island's successful eighty-six-year run was its location on the Ohio River, actually less because of the many easily accessible and enjoyable riverboats which took the visitors to and from the park, than because the Ohio River's spring floods ruined the park several times, demanding constant change and renovation and allowing for a newer and better park to be built after each flood. The park's most destructive flood was in 1937, when virtually the entire park was ruined. Edward

Schott, the owner of Coney Island and son of its original founder, rebuilt the park with steel foundations, curbing any further flood damage.

Schott always stressed cleanliness in Coney Island, making sure trash was never left lying around, and seeing that defacements and damages were promptly taken care of. So successful was he in his "clean amusement park" image that he was later chosen as one of the key men in the planning of Disneyland.

Strangely enough, Coney Island's

The Philadelphia Toboggan Company built 87 famous classic carousels, the most beautiful in the world. Number 17, at Riverview Park in 1915, is now located at Six Flags Over Georgia in Atlanta. (Chicago Historical Society)

success was the reason for its end. Due to its location on the river banks, it eventually ran out of expansion room and began having problems handling the large crowds that were increasing every year, and the Ohio River was still an ever-lurking menace. So in 1971 Coney Island's last owners, the Taft Broadcasting Company, closed the park and moved most of its rides and attractions to a new location just north of Cincinnati, where it was reopened in 1972 as Kings Island.

The popular Palisades Park was located in Fort Lee, New Jersey, on the banks of the Hudson River just across from midtown Manhattan. It began as a trolley park in 1897, and followed a parallel though smaller-scaled history of nearby Coney Island throughout the twentieth century. While Palisades Park didn't have the beach or as great an amusement variety to offer as Coney, its cleanliness, excitement, and convenient location for Manhattan and New Jersey dwellers was the main reason for its longevity.

Palisades Park was well known for the many gimmicks it would create as crowd-pullers, most famous of which were its beauty contests for every type of female imaginable, from Little Miss America to Miss Teenage America to Miss Polish America to Miss Fat America. One publicity stunt evolved when a young couple informed the management that they were going to be married and that they had the Palisades Park roller coaster to thank for it, as they met on that coaster. The park quickly decided that the couple would be married on the coaster, and they insisted on paying for the services and a honeymoon at Niagara Falls. The wedding was to be filmed as a newsreel and so had to be rehearsed sev-

eral times on the roller coaster, much to the dismay of the minister, who began turning several shades of green before the ceremony was complete.

For three-quarters of a century, the distant bright lights and fireworks of Palisades Park were a lovely and familiar sight for New Yorkers across the Hudson River, but by the 1960s the park wasn't making enough money to afford its expensive location in the Jersey Palisades. In 1971 its lease was bought out by the Centex-Winston Corporation, which quickly tore down Palisades Park and began building high-rise apartments.

Riverview Park in Chicago began in 1906, although for twenty-five years it had been operating as a picnic grove on

While the children in this Old Mill at Riverview Park are looking forward to being frightened in the dark, the couple in the background probably have more romantic plans. (Chicago Historical Society)

The Parachute Jump at Steeplechase Park was originally built in Queens for the 1939 World's Fair. (Brooklyn Public Library)

This is Riverview's Freak Show in 1960, at the beginning of the end of the park. (Chicago Historical Society, Photograph by Ray J. Spies)

the northern branch of the Chicago River. Riverview Park held the distinction of always presenting the newest and most exciting riding devices on its two-mile midway. One of its six roller coasters, the "Bobs," was the most popular ride in the park and was generally accepted as being the fastest roller coaster in the nation. It was finally topped in sales in 1959 by the park's newest roller coaster, the "Fireball," which dropped down 90 feet to a pile of rocks, ducking underneath them at the last second. The "Parachute Jump," introduced in 1937, was undoubtedly the park's most unique ride debut. In double-seated parachutes, passengers were slowly lifted up a tower

Despite Riverview Park's presence, the Chicago World's Fair of 1933 boasted a large midway. (James A. Payer Collection)

*Pittsburgh's Kennywood Park is still famous for its roller coasters.
This racer is one of the earlier ones in 1918.*

*A gentle boat row on the Kennywood
Park lagoon in 1920.*

220 feet high, from where they were dropped in a stomach-lunging descent. About 80 feet from the top, the parachute would billow out, slowing the descent and gently lowering the terrified couple to the ground. A 250-foot version of this ride was displayed at the New York World's Fair of 1939, after which it was transferred to Steeplechase Park, where it was in operation until 1966. So realistic was the Parachute Jump that the U.S. Armed Forces adopted it as training for its paratroopers.

Unfortunately, Riverview Park became the grounds for many gang and racial conflicts in the 1960s, and much of the city's population shied away from the

The "Bug House" at Kennywood Park in 1925 was a fun house
in the vein of George Tilyou's Pavilion of Fun.

In the late 1920s, many amusement parks had separate areas for children, with scaled-
down rides and children's shows. This kiddieland was in Kennywood Park.

Kennywood's midway in the late 1920s.

park's rough crowds. After a few years of having to flank the park with policemen, Riverview Park was forced to close down in 1969.

Like rain and fire, the bad reputation of amusement parks always was a thorn in the side of park owners. In the late 1920s, as the middle and upper classes of the nation's population bought their own cars, they began ignoring the trolley lines and their respective amusement parks. Amusement parks saw a drop in attendance, and several were no longer known as family entertainment parks but as hangouts for the local rowdies.

Playland, located at Rye, New York, on the northern shore of the Long Island Sound, was built in 1928 with the intention of keeping the family and "decent folk" in the amusement park. It was built by the Westchester County Department of Recreation on the site of what was known as Paradise Park, a pic-

Six Flags Over Texas.

nic ground that was the meeting place of every pickpocket, drunkard, and prostitute in Westchester County. The county wanted to rid itself of Paradise Park and at the same time design an amusement park which would satisfy the public's entertainment needs and supply picturesque surroundings. Playland's general manager, Frank Darling, worked on the theory that beautiful surroundings stimulate a beautiful mind, and the rowdiness of an ugly mind would thus be prevented.

When Playland opened in 1929, it presented itself as a handsome and perfectly designed park. Behind the entrance was a large mall lined with trees and flowerbeds, in the center of which stood a tower that provided the park with continuous recorded music. Picnic grounds and the children's ride area were separated from the noise of the major amusement area, and a beach was available for swimming and seaplane and speedboat rides over Long Island Sound.

Mr. Darling's theory proved to be a sound one, as hoodlums looking for trouble would enter the park and at first sneer at the surroundings, then begin to admire its beauty, and finally fall into the enchantment and pleasant atmosphere of Playland as they would have themselves an innocent good time.

It took constant work and expertise in amusement park management for Mr. Darling to keep any kind of trouble out of Playland, but his several prior years of experience on Coney Island taught him how to deal with sticky situations. For example, many of the more sober-minded of Playland's visitors began to complain of the wildness of the park's huge "Airplane Coaster," some of them even demanding that it be torn down. The coaster, Darling knew, was completely safe, but he decided to build a small and extremely gentle switchboard railway next to the coaster's entrance. In this way the genteel folk were diverted to the mild ride, and the

Playland's mall area in the 1930s. (Westchester County Playland Commission)

more adventuresome boarded the big coaster. This clever idea is used to this day in the nation's large parks: let the big rides and small rides feed on each other, and keep the crowds homogeneous and flowing smoothly through the park.

Playland became the model amusement park for the industry, an industry that was becoming concerned for the reputation and welfare of the amusement park as well as the acceptance of the amusement industry as a legitimate business. The filth and crime of a few ill-kept parks was blamed upon the whole industry. Some poorly maintained parks would often have ride accidents due to mechanical failure (most ride accidents are due to the stupid antics of the riders) which would also cause the whole industry to suffer. In 1922, an editorial appeared in the *Engineering News Record* which read:

> Just about thirty years ago the Chicago World's Fair gave birth to the mechanical "amusement device," which since then has come to infest every private park in the country and some public parks. During that time a record of accidents and fatalities has been piled up against these machines which characterizes them as not merely a public nuisance but a public menace. Two courses are open. If the thrill-making machines built for the alleged diversion of the working man and his family are held to satisfy a real need, they must be placed under such control . . . as will assure safety. . . . The other course is more radical but certain in its operation: Wipe out the amusement devices entirely. . . .

Such malignant written and verbal accusations were becoming common.

In 1920, during the American

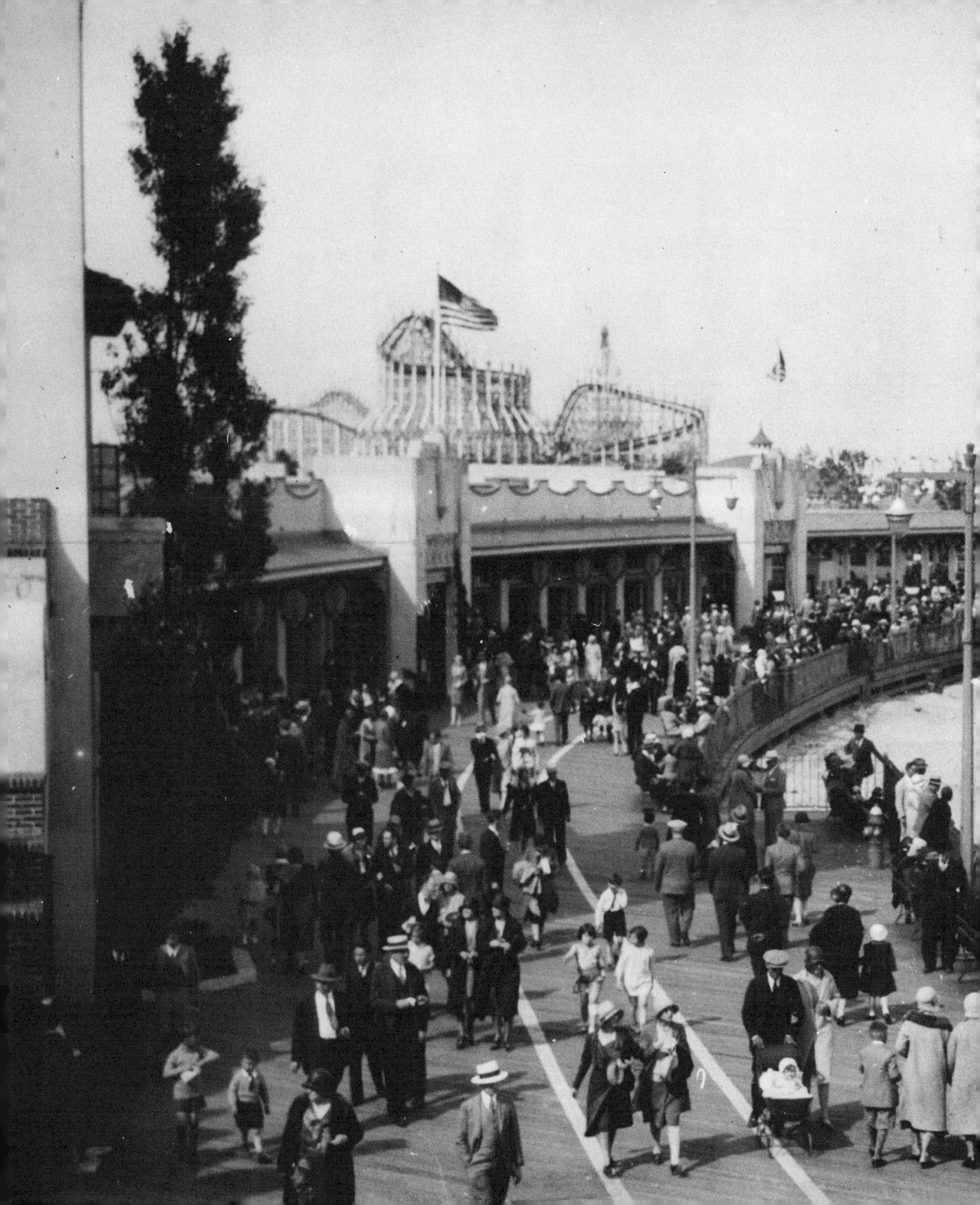

amusement-park peak, the International Association of Amusement Parks and Attractions was formed as a means of communication, exchange, safety, and self-protection for not only America's but the world's amusement parks. Now in its fifty-sixth year, the I.A.A.P.A. continues to hold annual conventions for its members, and to publish a monthly magazine which keeps park owners informed on how to maintain and improve their parks and what new advances in rides, equipment, and service have been made in the outdoor amusement industry.

The widespread use of the automobile in the 1920s meant the end of the trolley park, although not all amusement parks prior to then were built and operated by trolley companies. Hersheypark in Pennsylvania developed from—of all things—a chocolate bar. Milton S. Hershey had been in the candy business for several years when in 1903 he built a chocolate factory in south-central Pennsylvania, the home of the Pennsylvania Dutch. It took only a few short years for Hershey's chocolate to reach nationwide fame, enabling Hershey to found and expand the town of Hershey, of which Hersheypark became a part in 1907.

Youngstown, Ohio's Idora Park's swimming pool in 1926.

Idora Park's ballroom, shown in the 1930s, presented the very best of name band music.

The "Racer" at Cedar Point Park, Sandusky, Ohio, c. 1900. (James A. Payer Collection)

Cedar Point Park in the early 1960s, well on its way to becoming today's best traditional amusement park in the nation.

The "Octopus," shown here at Cedar Point Park in the 1950s, has long been a popular thrill ride, although today most parks have replaced it with the similar yet better "Monster" ride.

The Runaway Mine Train at Cedar Point Park today.

Geauga Lake Park, in Aurora, Ohio, started in 1872 as a camping, fishing, and picnicking site. The park is shown here c. 1920.

Geauga Lake Park was not a trolley park, and therefore had several bus lines available from the city.

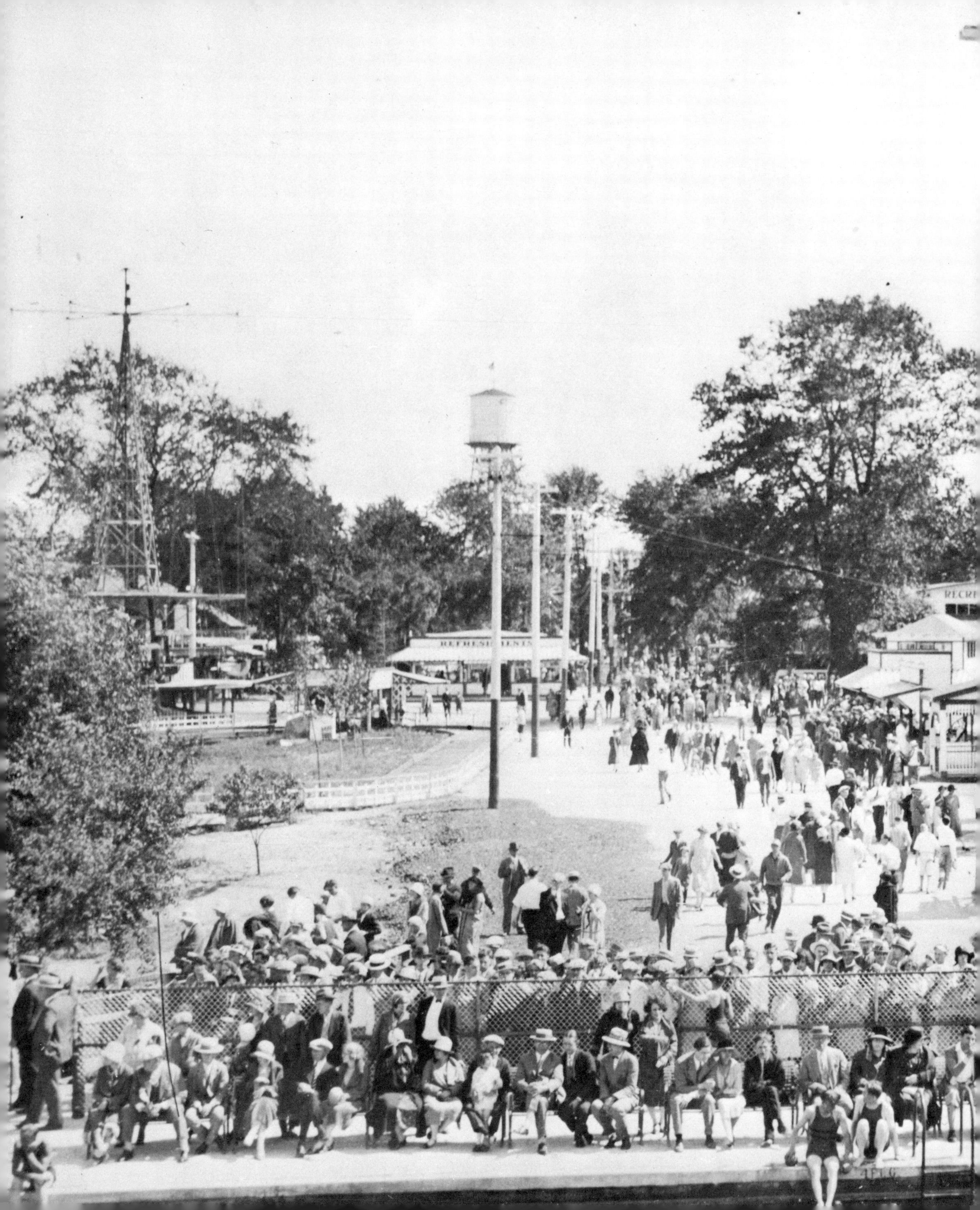

Johnny Weissmuller set the world record for the 220-yard freestyle in 1926 in Geauga Lake Park's swimming pool.

Geauga Lake Park's "Shooting Sky Rocket Coaster" was one of the world's longest coasters.

In 1920, the automobile was still an exciting novelty for Geauga Lake Park patrons.

Geauga Lake Park, seen here c. 1920, is still one of the nation's best traditional amusement parks.

Unlike most of the amusement parks of that time, Hersheypark was quiet and sedate, offering picnicking, boating, pleasant gardens, and musical festivals. Even when the outdoor swimming pool and the rides were later added one by one, Hersheypark remained unhurried. There was no need to push a Coney Island atmosphere onto Hersheypark in order to achieve success, as people came from miles around to visit the town of Hershey, tour the chocolate factory, and spend a relaxing afternoon in Hersheypark.

Throughout the years Hersheypark continued to grow with this mixture of fun and relaxation as it became a

127

This is not the landing of the original Mayflower, *but Spring Creek in Hersheypark c. 1910.*

The fun house at Hersheypark, c. 1950.

*The circular airplane ride at Hersheypark,
c. 1950.*

*The "Giant Wheel" offers a fine view of
modern Hersheypark.*

*The long-defunct Island Park in Easton, Pa.,
in 1905. (James A. Payer Collection)*

*The "Witching Waves" in Philadelphia's vanished Woodside Park consisted of a metal
floor whose wavelike action propelled passengers along its course. The original Witching
Waves was in Coney Island's Luna Park. C. 1905. (James A. Payer Collection)*

famed tourist spot. By 1973, the tourist trade was so heavy that tours through the chocolate plant became impossible. Instead, Chocolate World was built and opened in Hersheypark, giving visitors a free ride through a simulated story of how chocolate is made, from picking the beans off cocoa trees to the wrapping and shipping of a Hershey Chocolate Bar.

In the wake of the new trend towards amusement parks with themes, Hersheypark itself went through an impressive multimillion-dollar expansion program in 1973, completely altering its appearance by shedding its old picnic-grove face and becoming a bright new theme park. It was an unfortunate but necessary change, as the gardens and swimming pool could no longer accommodate the huge crowds.

Amusement parks in the American West were less dense and generally started a little later than parks in the East. One of the best and most beautiful of the Western parks is Elitch's Gardens in Denver. It began as an amusement park in 1916, although it had been a popular garden since 1890. Mary Elitch had had a large flower garden which began to attract the townspeople, who asked permission to look at her flowers. As more people began to visit her home, Mrs. Elitch decided to expand her gardens, add rare birds and animals, enclose the gardens with a fence, and open them to the public at a small fee. She soon added a band concert to her popular park, and in 1892 Elitch's Theater was opened and brought the great stage performers of Broadway to the appreciative Western audiences.

With the opening of the theater, Elitch's Gardens quickly became Denver's most popular entertainment spot. Townspeople rode out on summer eve-

The "Mountain Scenic Railway" c. 1905 in Philadelphia's Woodside Park. (James A. Payer Collection)

White City was a popular name for many eastern parks. This White City was in Syracuse, N.Y., c. 1900. (James A. Payer Collection)

Hersheypark's Sunken Gardens, c. 1953.

131

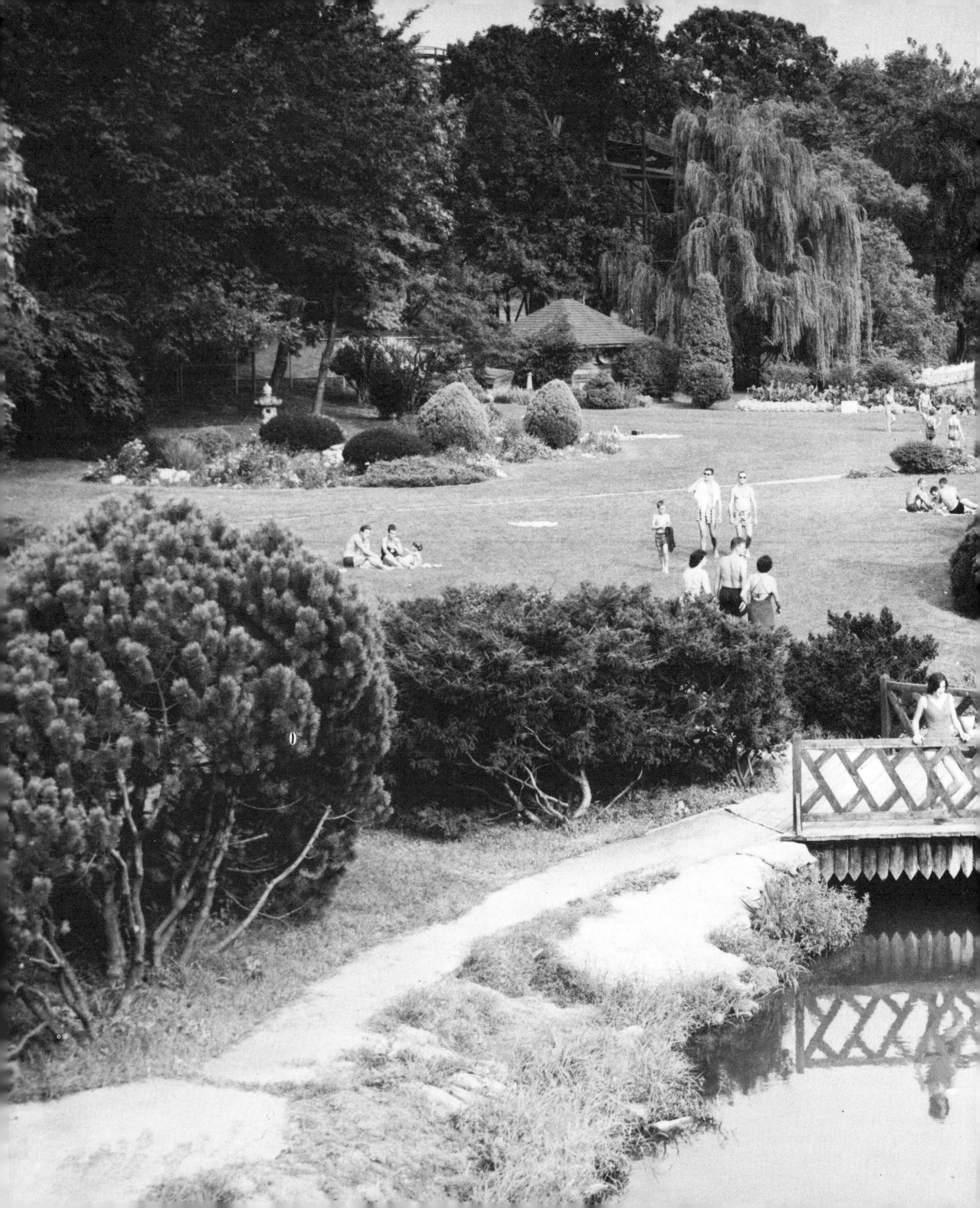

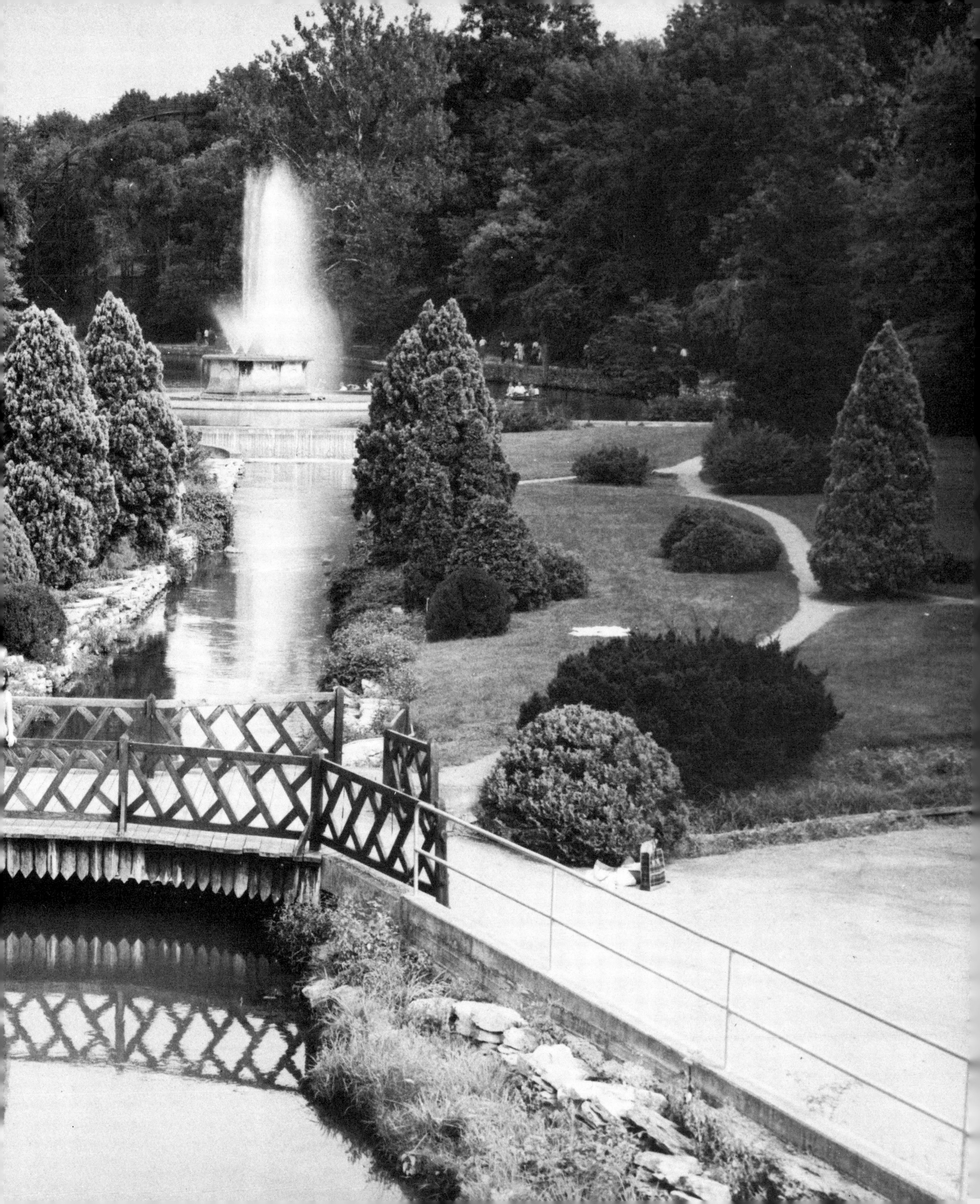

While it is actually located in Ontario, Crystal Beach, near Buffalo, N.Y., is generally considered an American amusement park. It is shown here in 1930. (James A. Payer Collection)

Crystal Beach in 1949. Today it is one of the nation's best traditional amusement parks.

Crystal Beach's "Cyclone," built in 1927, was generally believed to be the most frightening roller coaster ever built. A nurse was kept at the station to take care of fainters.

nings to watch the summer stock productions which over the years have included Douglas Fairbanks, Sarah Bernhardt, Cecil B. DeMille, Grace Kelly, Harold Lloyd, and Edward G. Robinson. The Trocadero Ballroom, or "The Troc," was added and began presenting the biggest-name bands of the day, including Benny Goodman, Glenn Miller, and Tommy Dorsey.

Although amusement rides were added to the Gardens in 1916, the emphasis on the garden atmosphere was maintained. As at Hersheypark, side shows and game barkers were prohibited, and orderly conduct was enforced. Men were not allowed on the dance floor without ties, and couples who began to swing too much to the band were at first monitored,

Carnival Park in Kansas City, 1906. (James A. Payer Collection)

Milwaukee's Pabst Park in 1904.
It grew out of a beer garden.
(James A. Payer Collection)

and then escorted off the dance floor. Today, Elitch's Gardens is still Denver's top resort, and the Elitch Theater is now America's oldest summer theater.

Southern California has had an illustrious history of amusement parks. In 1880, tobacco tycoon Abbott Kinney went there to visit what was the beginning of Los Angeles. Intrigued by the warm Mediterranean climate and anxious for a new business venture, Kinney decided to build Venice, the Riviera of the American West. In the area just south of what is now Santa Monica, Kinney constructed over 30 miles of Venetian canals; he built hotels, shops, theaters, and restaurants, all gilded with Roman arches, columns, and statues; he imported singing gondoliers from Italy, and he built a pier out over the ocean with a Spanish galleon restaurant and a large ballroom.

In short, Venice started out at the turn of the century as Coney Island had —as a sober, high-class resort. But Kinney's attempts to keep Venice a cultural center alive with opera, theater, and the refined arts proved futile, as Venice gradually became the Coney Island of Southern California. One by one, amusement-park piers were built and began surrounding Venice. Eventually the shriek of the sideshow barker began to drown out the singing gondolier, and the twisted frameworks of the roller coasters began to blot out the fine Italian architecture. From 1905 through 1912 a total of seven amusement-park piers were built along the 2-mile stretch of beach north and south of Venice. The three largest were Venice Amusement Pier, Ocean Park Pier, and Santa Monica Pier.

The most successful of the Venice piers was Ocean Park Pier. Opened in 1912, Ocean Park was one of the most attractive amusement parks of its time. It featured many new innovative rides, including the "Dodgem," now popularly known as "bumper cars." The pier was constantly plagued with fires, but like Cincinnati's Coney Island's floods, the fires enabled bigger and better Ocean Parks to be built. The last fire was in 1974, although the pier had been officially closed since 1968. Today, only the Santa Monica Pier remains, but its amusements are mostly gone. Abbott Kinney's "Riviera of the American West" is long gone, and only a few muddy canals and crumbling arches and columns are to be found in the now-residential city of Venice.

Thirty miles south of Venice in Long Beach, California, is The Pike, an oceanside amusement park. It was built in the 1880s with the same mature attitude of Venice and Coney Island, but it too soon succumbed to the no-pretense carny and ballyhoo fashion so well loved by the everyday American, and it continued as a prototype of the good old American amusement park. Because of its proximity to the motion-picture industry, The Pike has been used as a backdrop in almost every American motion picture using an amusement-park setting. Its colossal racer roller coaster, the "Cyclone Racer," was used as a prop for the comedy or dramatic climaxes of dozens of motion pictures, as stars like Eddie Cantor, Kim Novak, Lou Costello, Anne Bancroft, Cameron Mitchell, and even the Beast from 20,000 Fathoms found themselves perched on its treacherous heights.

The Pike was renamed the Nu-Pike in the fifties, and again renamed Queen's Pike in 1968, when Great Britain's *Queen Mary* found her permanent berth in Long Beach Harbor. Today, Queen's Pike has deteriorated considerably, and is just a depressing shadow of what The Pike used to be. It is more than likely that it will soon be torn down in order to make way for expensive shops and restaurants in the beach renovation program brought on by the *Queen Mary's* regal presence.

In San Francisco, George Whitney was the owner of Playland-at-the-Beach, the world's largest privately owned amusement park. Whitney built Play-

This scenic railway was at New Orleans' West End in 1901. Both West End and Old Spanish Fort came to an end when Pontchartrain Beach Amusement Park opened in 1928. (The Historic New Orleans Collection)

Electric Park at Galveston, Texas, 1905. (James A. Payer Collection)

Elitch's Gardens is still a successful combination of lovely gardens and exciting rides.

Denver's Lakeside Amusement Park, shown here in 1907, still enjoys success along with Elitch's Gardens. (James A. Payer Collection)

land-at-the-Beach in the 1920s, although he had already been in the amusement business for several years, working at several different parks and making a few inventions. He invented the Photo-While-You-Wait Booth, the cartoon cutouts in which people stick their heads for character photos, and the Jumbo Hot Dog.

Whitney was like George Tilyou; he had a keen talent for attracting customers, but not cheating them. Also like Tilyou, Whitney didn't believe P. T. Barnum's philosophy that "there's a sucker born every minute." He therefore allowed no ballyhoo in Playland-at-the-Beach, staffing his concessions instead with young employees working on salary. Prizes for the games were coupons redeemable at the merchandise store. The profit was made on the prizes, not the games. Like most park owners, Whitney's most popular prize was the Kewpie doll, of which he bought 300,000 a year from a

Elitch's Theater.

Lagoon, c. 1908.

San Francisco man who made the little plaster dolls in his basement at a cost of four cents each.

Playland-at-the-Beach ran successfully until the early 1950s, after which it began dropping off in attendance due mostly to the dismantling of the park's two biggest attractions: the Shoot-the-Chutes and the Big Dipper roller coaster. Roller coasters have always been the biggest money-makers for amusement parks, and it is common knowledge that the bigger the coaster, the better the park. Several parks have suffered drastically when their coasters have been dismantled for one reason or another (usually because of highway developments) and many of them eventually folded. But while a roller coaster is the biggest money-maker, it is also the biggest expense and headache. Maintenance costs can average as high as $10,000 to $15,000 a year, not to mention fire insurance and protection against the idiots who stand up during the ride and are killed. At Playland-at-the-Beach, George Whitney had a $400,000 annual insurance policy protecting him from such idiots, but its huge premiums began to prove uneconomical, and the Big Dipper and the Shoot-the-Chutes were both torn down, sealing the park's fate.

Amusement Parks Cross Country in Pictures

Located north of Salt Lake City, Lagoon Amusement Resort was started in 1896 to promote business on the Salt Lake and Ogden railroad.

Lagoon, c. 1915. The park is still enjoying great success.

Venice just after the turn of the century.

The peaceful serenity of the Venice canals.

This mild amusement section in 1910 on the Venice shorefront was only a prelude to what was to come. (Los Angeles County Museum of Natural History)

Fraser's Million-Dollar Pier, 1912.

Looking south towards Fraser's Million-Dollar Pier, Santa Monica, California.

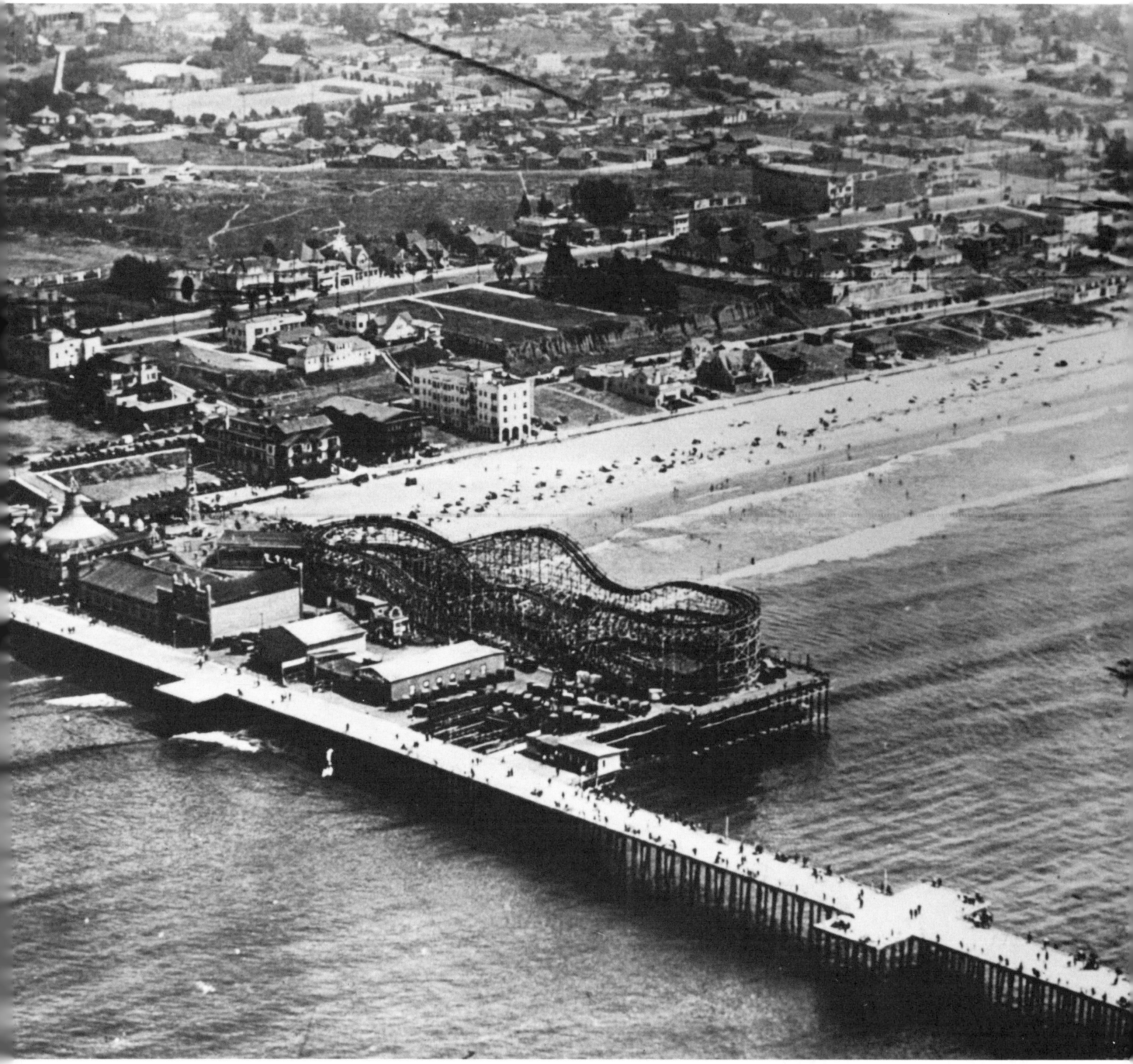

The Santa Monica Pier, 1914.

Santa Monica Pier in the 1920's. Food was cheaper then.
(Ken Strickfaden Collection)

Venice Amusement Pier, 1922. (Ken Strickfaden Collection)

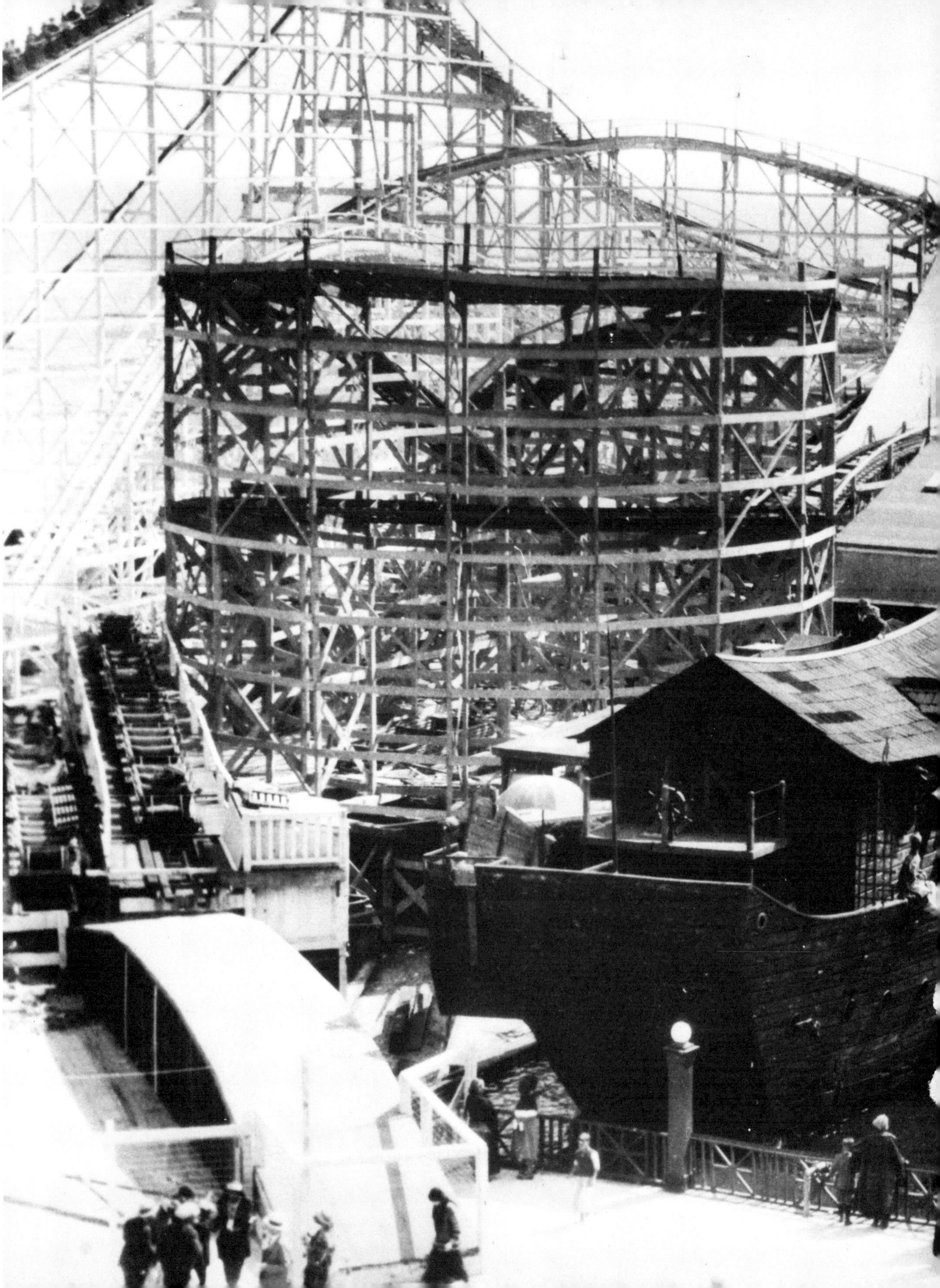

Venice Amusement Pier, 1922. (Ken Strickfaden Collection)

The Ocean Park .fire of 1924. (Ken Strickfaden Collection)

Looking south along The Pike in its heyday in the 1940s.

*The Venice Amusement Pier midway, showing the 120-foot "Bamboo Slide."
(Ken Strickfaden Collection)*

Ashes to ashes, dust to dust, but nothing stopped amusement parks, then, as Ocean Park Pier was rebuilt in 1925. (Ken Strickfaden Collection)

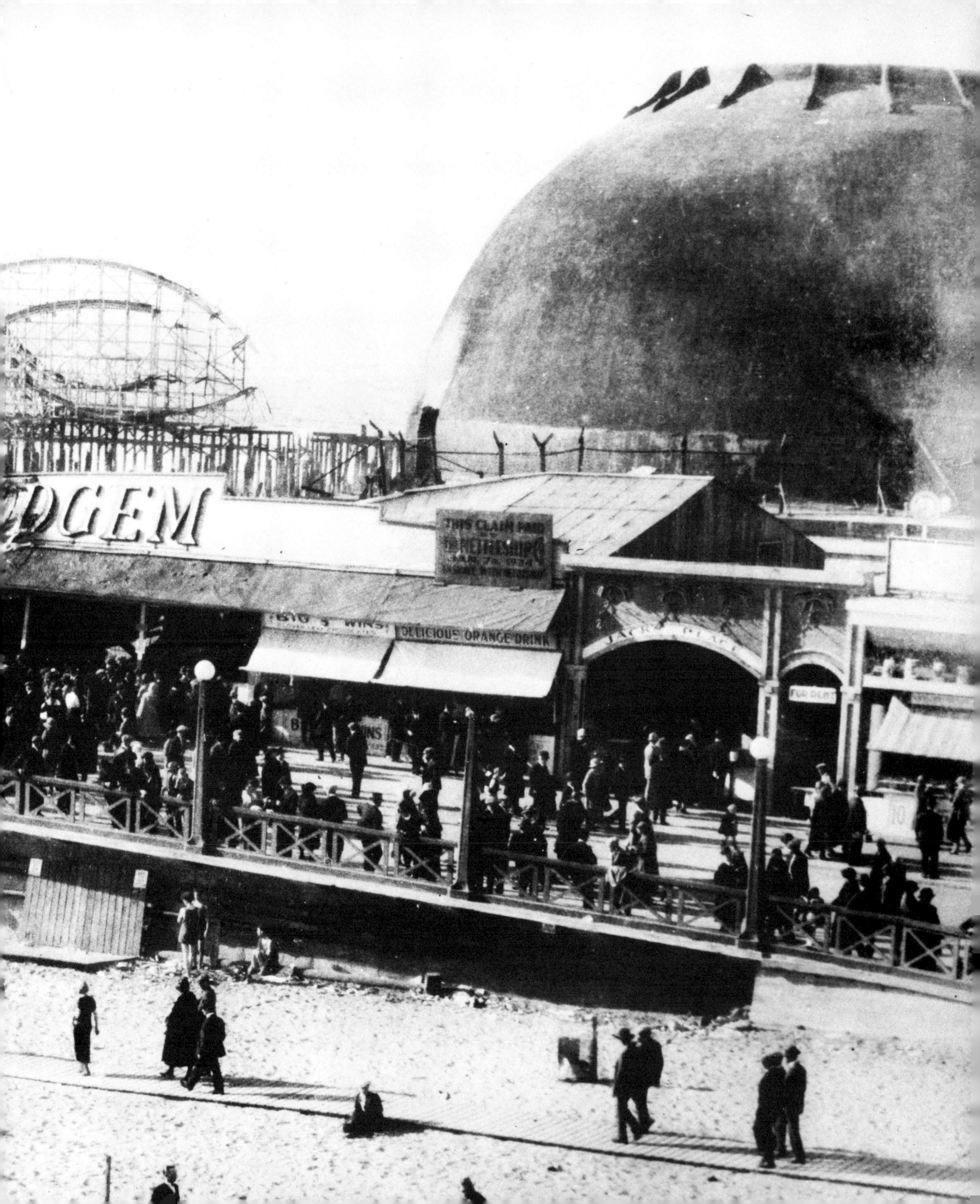
DGEM
DELICIOUS ORANGE DRINK
FOR RENT

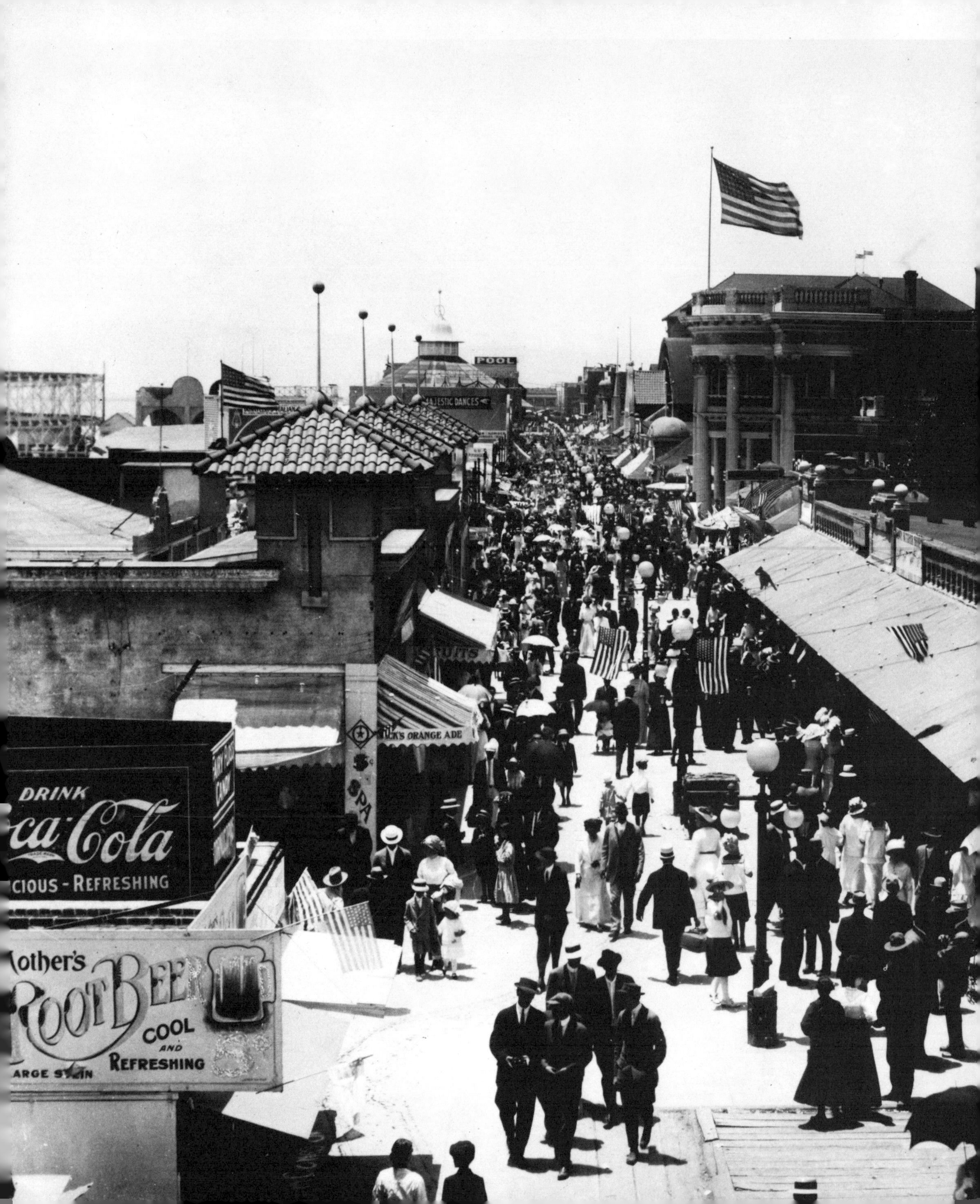
POOL
JESTIC DANCES
ORANGE ADE
DRINK
ca-Cola
CIOUS - REFRESHING
Mother's
ROOT BEER
COOL
AND
REFRESHING
ARGE 5¢ TIN
SPA

Looking north along the Long Beach Pike in 1905. (Los Angeles County Museum of Natural History)

The Pike was still going strong in the 1950s.

The Pike in the early 1950s.

The Pike in the late 1950s.

The Pike's "Cyclone Racer" was removed in 1968 because of highway development.

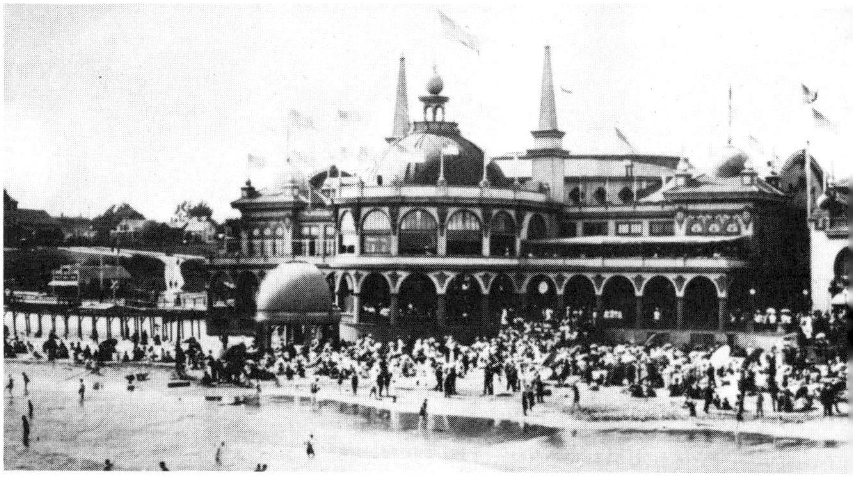

Queen's Pike today.

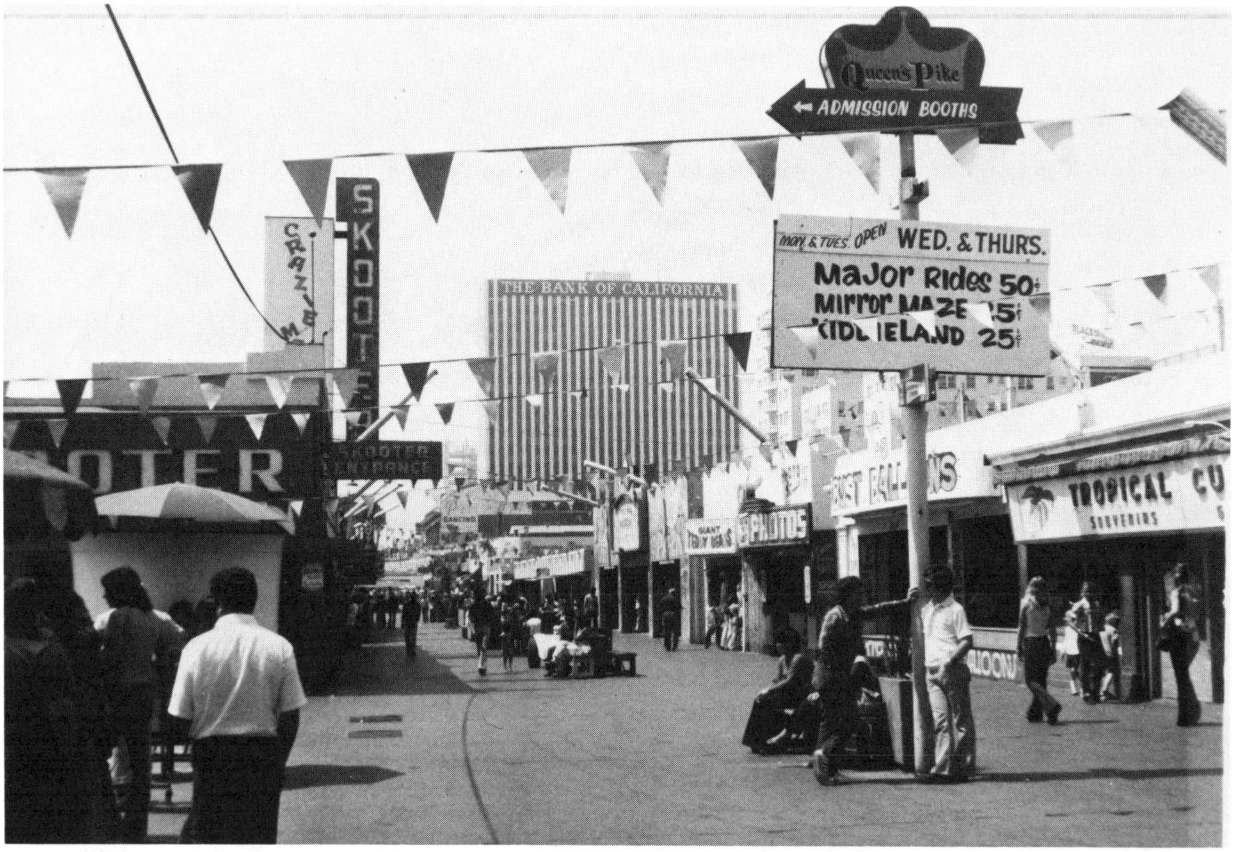

Queen's Pike
ADMISSION BOOTHS
WED. & THURS.
Major Rides 50¢
THE BANK OF CALIFORNIA
TROPICAL
SOUVENIRS
PHOTOS

This is Santa Cruz Beach's second casino and indoor plunge in 1911. The amusements were developed quickly afterwards.

Santa Cruz, California, built its first beach casino in 1904, as it is seen here. It burned down in 1905.

San Francisco's Playland-at-the-Beach in the late 1930s. (The Blaisdell Collection)

Playland-at-the-Beach was expanded by 50 percent in the 1940s. (The Blaisdell Collection)

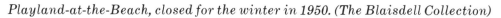

Playland-at-the-Beach, closed for the winter in 1950. (The Blaisdell Collection)

The long-departed Luna Park in Seattle, Washington, 1906. (James A. Payer Collection)

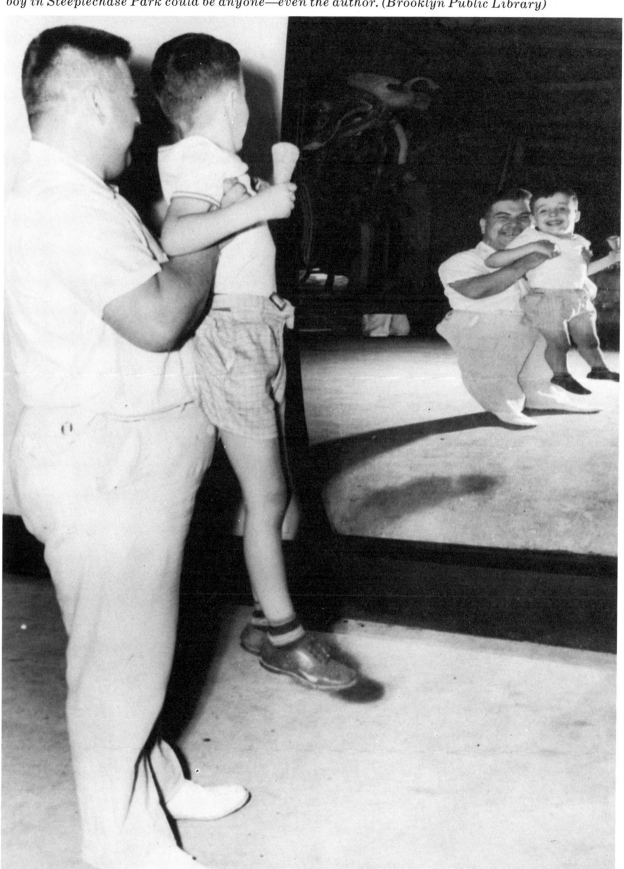

In the amusement parks, the only faces that don't change are the children's. This little boy in Steeplechase Park could be anyone—even the author. (Brooklyn Public Library)

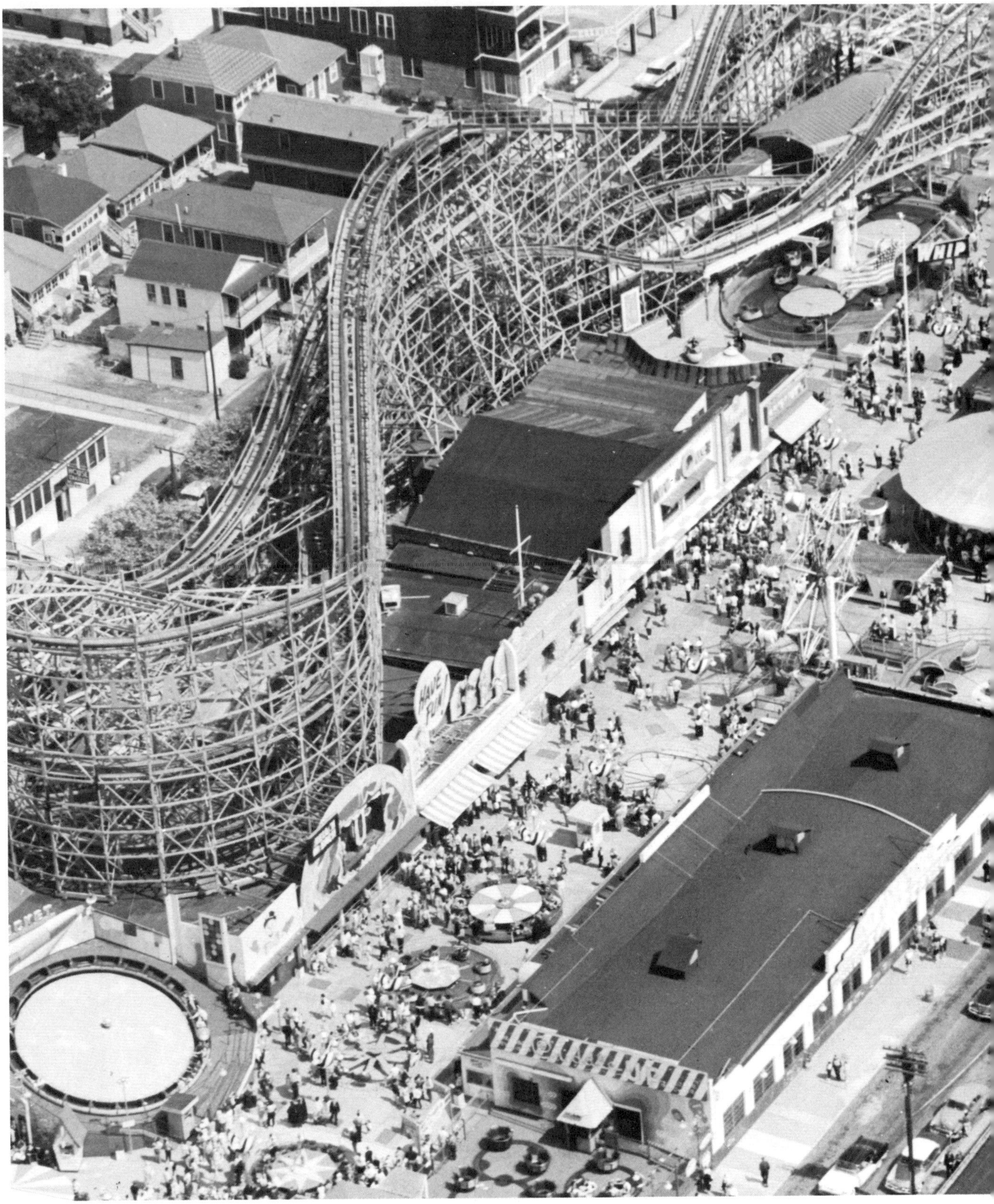
WHIP
HAVE FUN!

Rockaway's Playland on Long Island in New York is one of the less than 100 American amusement parks which have maintained themselves successfully from the early part of the century to the present. Rockaway's Playland is shown here in the 1950s.

By the 1930s, several amusement parks had closed, and by 1936, the 1,500 amusement parks of 1919 had shrunk to about 500. The two major reasons for the falloff were the widespread use of the automobile and the Depression. But the 1940s showed a substantial rise in the industry. While few new parks were built during the early 1940s, the 200 large parks which were still operating were doing a handsome business. Americans were on a post-Depression and World War II spending spree, and the weather was good for five straight seasons. The banner year in the outdoor amusement industry was 1946, as Americans and Canadians spent over $100,000,000 riding Ferris wheels, playing skee-ball, eating cotton candy, and generally having the time of their lives.

New amusement parks were being planned again in the late 1940s, but the television craze of the early 1950s put people back into their homes, and the amusement industry, right along with the motion picture industry, suddenly looked bleak again. There is one man, however, who in the 1950s gave the American amusement park the great push it needed and saved it from what looked like extinction—Walter Elias Disney.

Sleeping Beauty's Castle during Disneyland's 1954 construction.
(Delmar Watson, Watson Family Archives)

ALONG WITH HIS FAME as the father of Mickey Mouse—an American institution as great as the hot dog and roller coaster—Walt Disney is considered in the amusement park business to be the revolutionist of the American amusement park. Disneyland had been a dream of his for several years before he announced, in 1954, his plans for the 180-acre Southern California park. Disney planned a park which would incorporate his famous cartoon characters and animated and feature films with historical lore, Americana, and a look at the world of tomorrow. As a contract between Walt Disney Productions and ABC-TV (which included the simultaneous beginning of the weekly television show, "Disneyland"), the "Magic Kingdom" was to be divided into five sections: Main Street, U.S.A., the American City at the turn of the century; Adventureland, consisting of the wilds of Africa; Frontierland, the American West of the 1800s; Fantasyland, complete with Mickey Mouse, Snow White, Peter Pan and the gang; and Tomorrowland.

Walt Disney stressed the idea of using themes in order to unify and structure a park more carefully. He felt that people would be more inclined to rides and attractions which revolve around a specific historical, cultural, or geographical theme, and it would keep the park more organized and attractive. When the plans for the $10,000,000 park were announced, park owners and enthusiasts were doubtful of Disneyland's success. This "theme park," as the new term popped up, was to contain only two rides (a carousel and a miniature train) which were close to a typical amusement park ride (no roller coaster, no Ferris wheel, no bumper cars or tunnels-of-love), there were to be no games of skill or chance, and, breaking an unwritten law of the industry, the park didn't even border on a large body of water. But after Disneyland's well-publicized opening in June 1955, the park began presenting staggering attendance figures, averaging over 5,-000,000 visitors a year since.

Families who shied away from the dirty carny atmosphere of some of the older, and by now gone, amusement parks began visiting Disneyland in the millions. They rode a horse-drawn streetcar down Main Street, took a jungle river cruise through the African rivers of Adventureland, rode a sternwheel steamboat down the Mississippi River in Frontierland, flew on Dumbo the Flying Elephant in Fantasyland, and experienced an updated version of A Trip to the Moon in Tomorrowland. As repeat visits to the park proved excessive, and the "Disneyland" television show rushed into the top ten of the television ratings, it became certain: Disneyland was an unparalleled success.

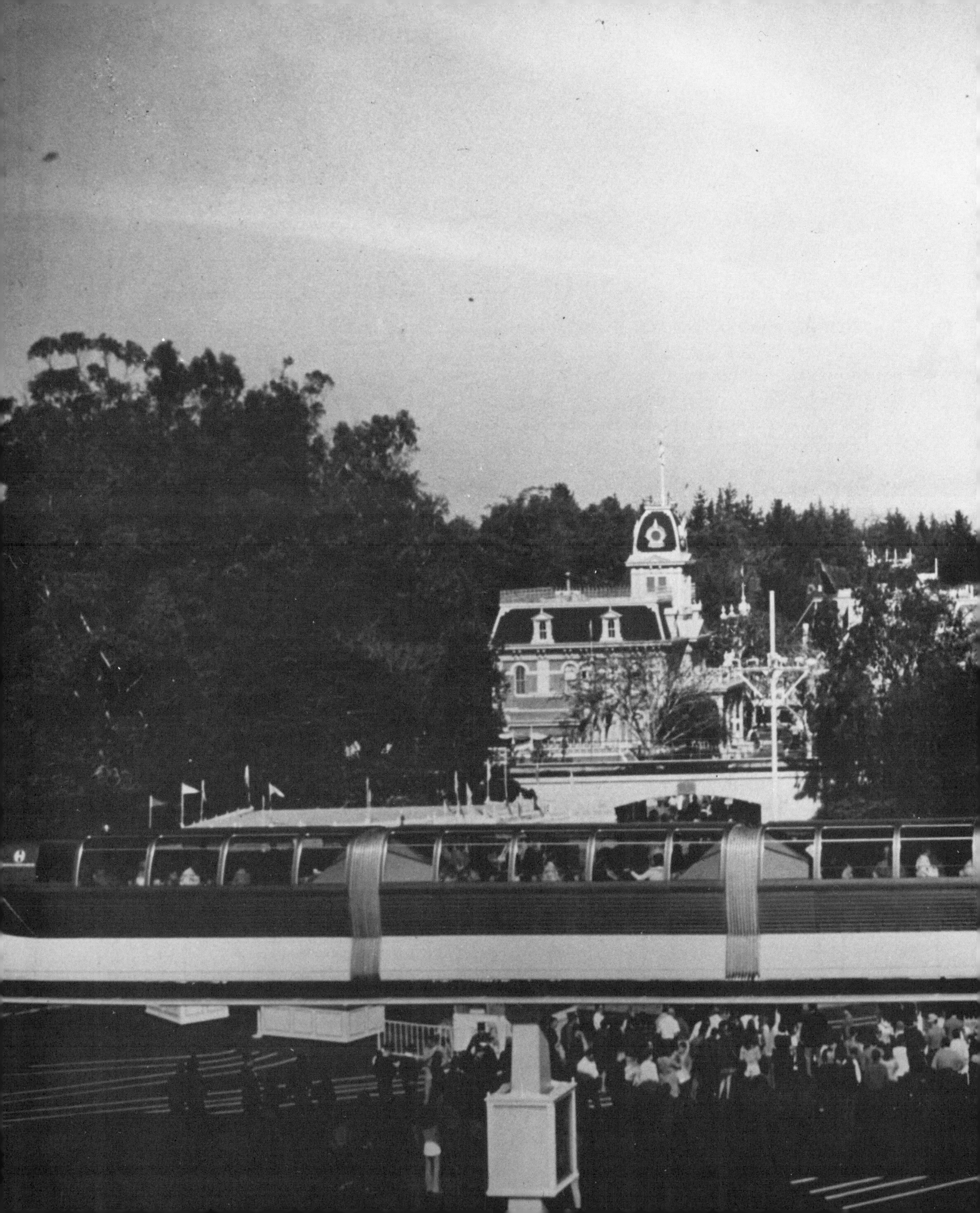

The Disneyland–Alweg Monorail system was the world's first. (© Walt Disney Productions)

No, this is not a trolley park, but the Town Square of Main Street, U.S.A., in Disneyland. (© Walt Disney Productions)

Walt Disney's statement that Disneyland would never be completed holds true to this day, as newer and bigger attractions are presented each year. In 1959, the park had one of its biggest additions as it added a 146-foot replica of the Matterhorn Mountain, complete with bobsleds racing down its icy slopes to a splash in a glacier lake, a submarine ride, boasting the fourth largest fleet of submarines in the world, and the world's first monorail system. Other major attractions, among a total of 55 in this almost unbelievable park, include a train ride over a desert complete with animated wildcats, rattlesnakes, and coyotes, an adventure-filled Tom Sawyer's Island, the Tomorrowland

Easily the most popular attractions in Disneyland are the speedy "Matterhorn Bobsleds."
(© Walt Disney Productions)

Disney's Audio-Animatronics are obviously seventy years ahead of Thompson and Dundy's illusionary thrills. This is a scene from Disneyland's spectacular Pirates of the Caribbean. (© *Walt Disney Productions*)

This is Ocean View Park in 1954, before the change to Pacific Ocean Park.
(James A. Payer Collection)

Autopia—a super-freeway on which visitors drive small gasoline-powered cars, and the Golden Horseshoe Revue, a wild barroom vaudeville show in the Old West. More recently, the Disney-produced Audio-Animatronics presents electronic and incredibly lifelike people and animals who are the stars of multimillion-dollar productions such as the "Haunted Mansion," the "Pirates of the Caribbean," and the rollicking "Country Bear Jamboree."

In short, Disneyland is a modern version of Coney Island's Luna and Dreamland parks, but it is obvious that the world-famous Disney park will be around a lot longer than Dreamland was. Disneyland, in its evergrowing, ever-changing, ever-pleasing entertainment, stands as a fitting monument to Walt Disney.

In the 1957 wake of Disneyland's success and the new type of "theme amusement park" (we will call the older parks "traditional amusement parks") that was proven to be a money-maker, plans were started for several prototype parks of Disneyland at various locations in the United States. A Disneyland spokesman at that time estimated that twenty parks modeled after Disneyland would appear in the U.S. within the next five years. He was way off in his guess, as only a handful of the plans materialized. Denver's Magic Mountain (not to be confused with the currently successful Southern California theme park), was one of the first attempts. Scheduled for a 1958 opening, its

Pacific Ocean Park in 1958. It was too lavish for
its own good and ended in bankruptcy.

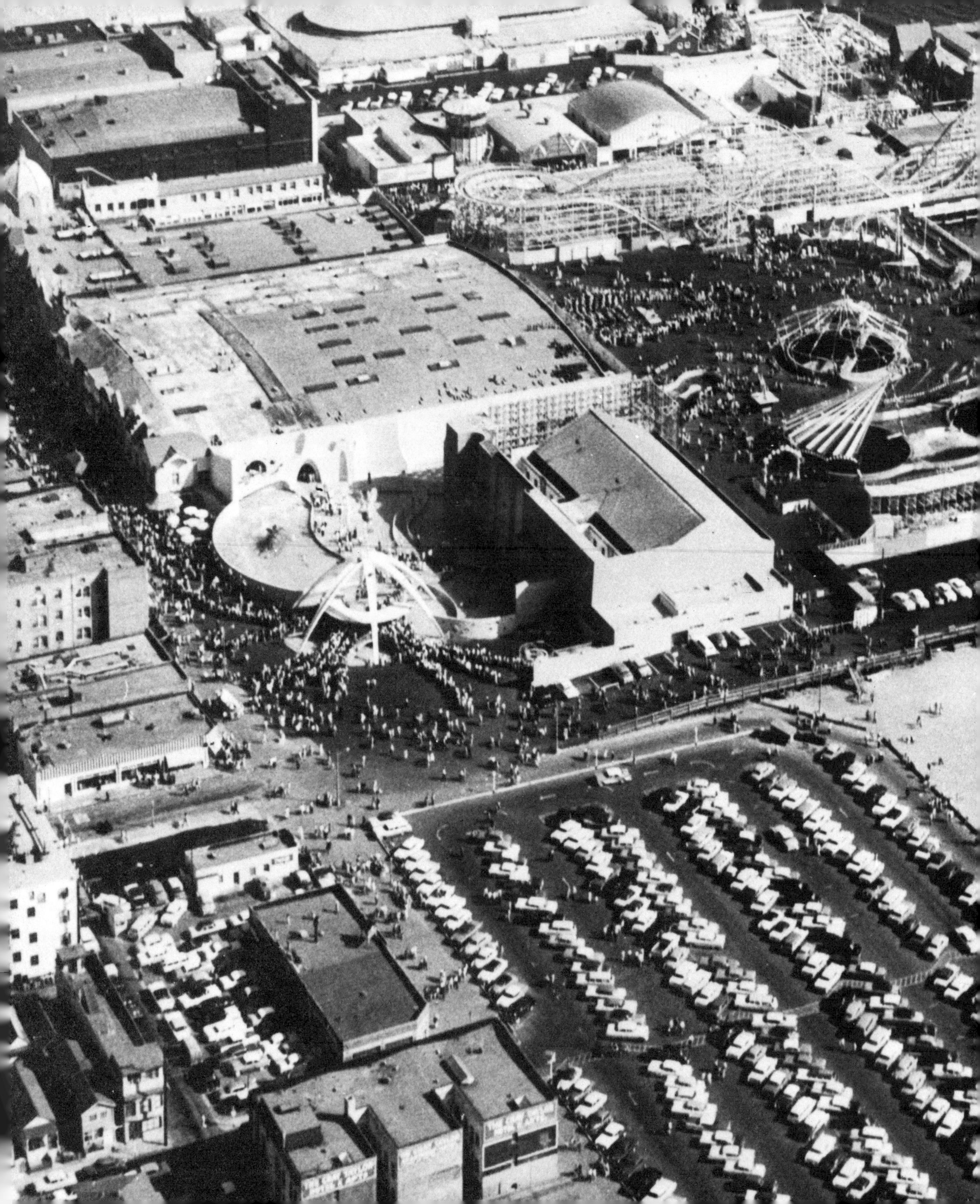

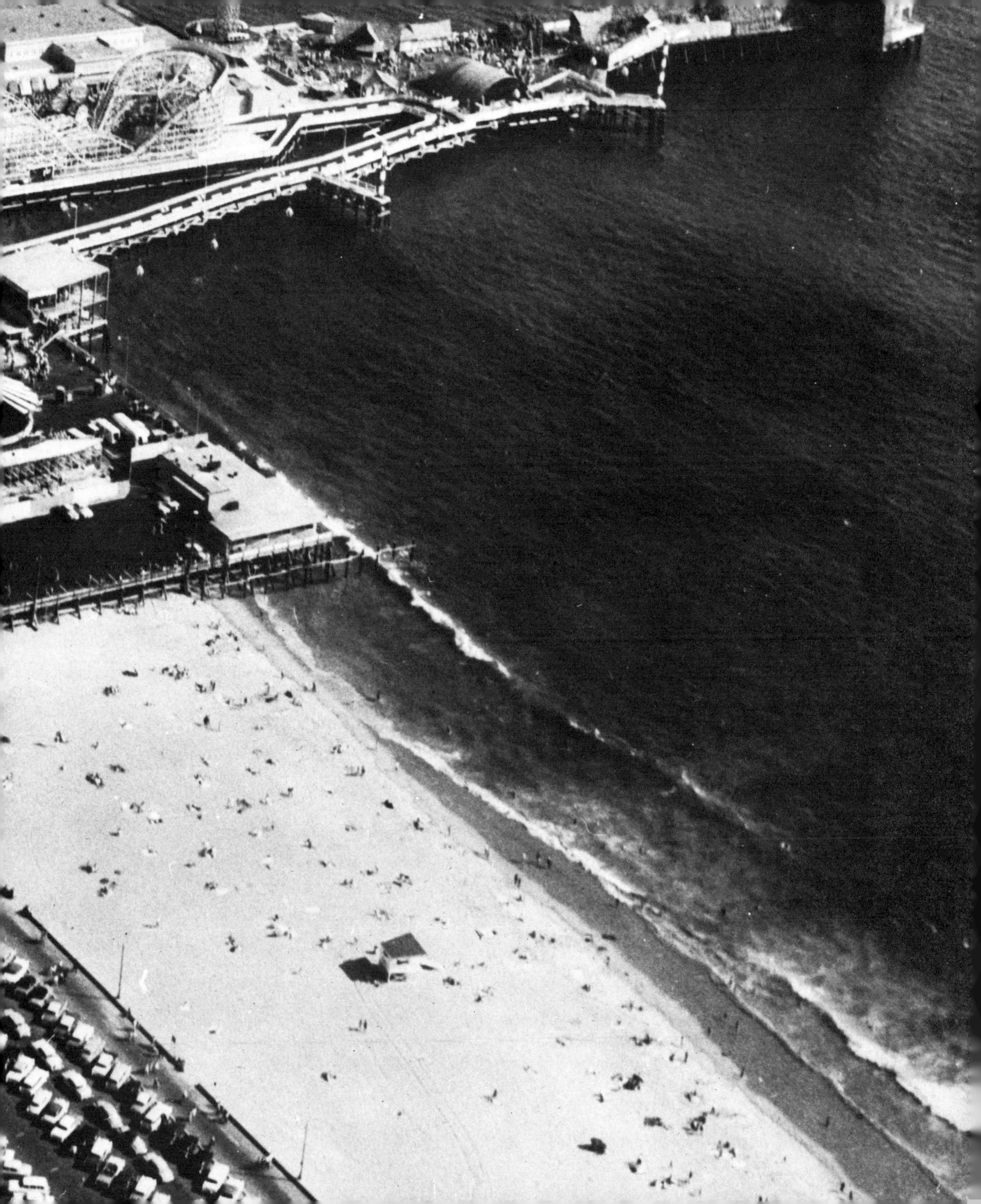

Sixty-five years after Paul Boyton's Sea Lion Park—performing seals at Pacific Ocean Park. (James A. Payer Collection)

The "Ocean Bubbles" at Pacific Ocean Park. (James A. Payer Collection)

attractions were to include a cable-car ride to the top of a mountain, a boatride on a man-made Colorado River, a shoot-'em-up Western town, an Old West train ride, and a few other less outstanding versions of Disneyland's original attractions. However, due to a gross overexpenditure in promotion and a lack of enthusiastic backers, the park never opened, and construction never went further than a few buildings. The Denver residents never felt a loss, as they continued to patronize Denver's two big parks, Lakeside Amusement Park and Elitch's Gardens, both of which are still successful today.

Another unsuccessful theme park which opened in 1959 was Pleasure Island, at Wakefield, Massachusetts, near Boston. This $4,000,000 80-acre park was to include a Pirates Island, a Western town called Cactus Flats, and Engine City, with the history of transportation. The main feature of Pleasure Island was to be a whaling port, with whaling boat rides in search of Moby Dick, a 70-foot replica of the giant whale which would rear up out of the water. Not only did this mammoth apparition prove inoperative, but the entire park failed in its theme attempt, and thrill rides had to be added in order to attract the crowds. Today, Pleasure Island is still operating as a small traditional amusement park.

The first successful, though short-lived, theme park was Pacific Ocean Park in

A dart game at Pacific Ocean Park.

Santa Monica, California. It had actually started as Ocean Park in 1950, standing on the same pier on which the old Ocean Park had stood until it was torn down in 1947. The park operated as a traditional amusement park until 1958, when it was bought by the Hollywood Turf Club and CBS-TV. Realizing the new trend toward theme parks, the new owners completely redesigned the park at a cost of $16,000,000 to give it a marine theme, and the new Pacific Ocean Park was opened in July 1958. P.O.P., as it was nicknamed, was one of the most exciting and original amusement parks ever built, with rides and attractions almost as innovative as Disneyland's. Visitors entered the park through Neptune's Kingdom, a torrent of waterfalls, whirlpools, and mermaids. Once inside, they could watch the Sea Circus, a 2,000-seat amphitheater presenting trained sea animals, view the ocean depths through the Double Diving Bell, ride a glass "water bubble" out over the Pacific Ocean, take a "Flight to Mars," ride the "Sea Serpent Roller Coaster" or any of the other thrill rides cleverly designed to match the ocean

Old Chicago in Freedomland, U.S.A.

theme. P.O.P's biggest attraction was its South Sea Island, with a banana train ride through a tropical storm, into a volcanic crater with erupting geysers, and climaxing in a cavern with a catastrophic earthquake.

But Pacific Ocean Park suffered a strange fate in that it was too large and had too many rides and attractions for its own good. With a single admission charge of $2.50 that entitled the guest to all of the rides and shows he wanted (except the roller coaster, which cost twenty-five cents), the park could not maintain its huge operation. With such a high overhead and a low income, something had to give somewhere. In P.O.P.'s case it was maintenance, and as it deteriorated against the rough ocean elements, the crowds stopped coming. When the park closed due to bankruptcy in 1968, it looked as if it had aged fifty years instead of just ten.

The most disastrous of the theme parks, and probably the most disastrous of any amusement park, was Freedomland, U.S.A., in The Bronx, New York, one half hour from

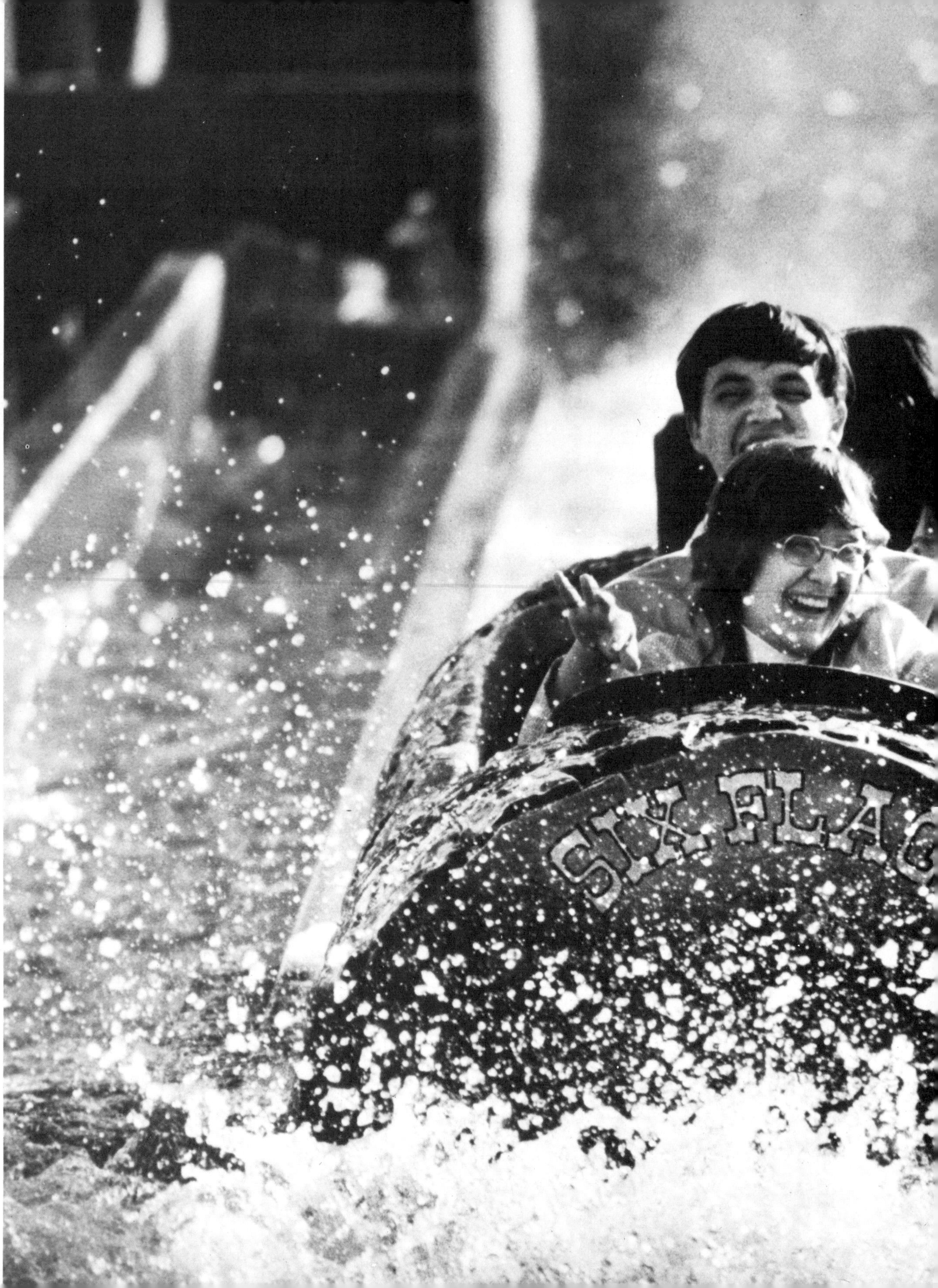
SIX FLAG

Six Flags Over Texas:
Getting wet
was never such a thrill.

The changing of the Pony Express riders at Freedomland, U.S.A.

Manhattan. At a cost of $33,000,000, "the World's largest outdoor family entertainment center" was opened in June 1960 and was advertised as the park that would be the Disneyland of the East. The park was shaped like the United States and its theme was U.S. history. Its publicity department claimed: "By re-creating the scope of the American Adventure, Freedomland brings history to life, makes an educational experience vastly entertaining."

Freedomland's major attractions were Little Old New York in 1850, with horse-drawn streetcars and tugboat rides around the New York harbor; New England, with fishing villages, whaling ports and a 1909 Cadillac car ride; a stern-wheeler around the Great Lakes; the Chicago fire; a Santa Fe train robbery; a fur-trapper ride through the Northwest Passage; San Francisco's Chinatown and earthquake; Civil War battle-grounds, and a New Orleans Mardi Gras. Like Disneyland, there were no thrill rides, but unlike Disneyland, there was a lack of that indefinable "magic" which only Disney seems to produce in theme parks. A successful amusement park, theme or traditional, must have either thrills or exciting shows, or "magic," in order to continue drawing its customers. Freedomland, U.S.A., had none of these.

On its opening day, 60,000 people stormed Freedomland's gate, over twice the number expected. They walked through a half-completed park that didn't entertain or educate them. Guests would watch the Pony Express riders change horses or firemen put out a burning building in Chicago (no live people this time), and then shrug and go on, wondering if anything better would be in another part of this micro-America. The spreading word-of-mouth that accompanies the opening of any amusement park said

The Runaway Mine Train at Six Flags Over Texas.

only that the park was one big bore, not worth the $3.50 admission. A few days after the opening, a stagecoach overturned in the park and injured ten people. This well-publicized accident seemed to predict Freedomland's early failure as its attendance abruptly dropped.

After running in the red for three seasons and realizing the failure of the park's attempt, Freedomland did an almost complete reversal for the 1963 season, removing all of the expensive theme attractions except for two dark rides, and filling the park up with thrill rides. The San Francisco section was entirely blocked off, and the personnel was cut almost in half, removing the costumed people who roamed around their respective theme areas, performing in shows or otherwise creating atmosphere. But both tightening up the overhead and changing into a thrill rides park were too late to save the doomed Freedomland. After losing over $5,000,000 a year, Freedomland, U.S.A. was forced to close down in 1964, to the disappointment of no one.

The first theme park to really start the mushrooming of non-Disneyland theme parks was Six Flags Over Texas, located on a 35-acre site between Fort Worth and Dallas. It was built by real estate developer Angus Wynne, and was opened in the spring of 1961.

Six Flags' planners and designers thought of showing the Texas history by the succession of flags whose ruling they represented: Spain, France, Mexico, the Republic of Texas, the Confederacy, and the United States. Around a 300-foot lookout tower designed like a Texas oil derrick, Six Flags is divided into six sections, with each historical segment as the motif for each section. Under the Spanish flag, visitors can ride the

The "Great American Scream Machine" roller coaster at Six Flags Over Georgia.

Spanish rapids in a huge hollowed-out log; in France they can ride a riverboat with LaSalle; in Mexico they ride on a train whose roofs consist of huge sombreros and which takes them through Old Mexico; in the Republic of Texas Judge Roy Bean himself enforces the law, complete with holdups and shootouts; in the Confederacy they can ride a wild runaway mine train, and in the United States they can ride an even wilder American roller coaster. The park abounds with shows, with French girls doing the cancan, a country and Western hootenanny, an opera house, and popular music. And the whole park has ample shading from the hot Texas sun with trees that hold over 100 electric fans, and awnings with air conditioning. A single admission price at the gate covers all of the park's rides, shows, and attractions.

The Six Flags Over Texas flew so high that Six Flags, Inc., was formed, and a Six Flags park chain was started that now includes Six Flags Over Georgia, near Atlanta, and Six Flags Over Mid-America, near St. Louis.

When Six Flags Over Texas began raking in the money, the race was on for theme parks to start in every available and economically sound area of the U.S. These new theme parks all share the same basic formula. They are split up into six or seven different areas, with a specific theme as the motif for each area. Careful attention is paid to the parks' design and placement of rides, shows, and attractions. The rides are all high capacity and are spaced apart to keep crowds from gathering in a particular spot. Shops and restaurants (either sit-down or fast-food) are conspicuously placed at the entrance/exit and in between rides and attractions, giving them more business from crowds coming and going from one to another.

Cleanliness is the number-one rule at theme parks, and the staff consists basically of cheerful, well-scrubbed young people of high school or college age. A single admission price is charged at the gate, ranging from $5.00 to $8.50 for adults, and all of the rides, shows, and attractions are included in the one price.

But unlike the Disney park, the rides in the new theme parks are basically thrill rides, including from twenty to thirty major rides and ten to fifteen kiddie rides. The same rides, slightly disguised to fit each park's theme, can usually be found in all the theme parks. The most popular rides, besides the ever-popular standard roller coaster (which now costs $2,000,000 to $3,000,000 to build), are the flume ride or log ride, a modern version of the old shoot-the-chutes, and the "Runaway Mine Train," a mild family version of the roller coaster. Both of these rides are produced by the Arrow Development Company in California, which is now also producing the "Corkscrew," a modern high-capacity version of the 1901 Loop-the-Loop.

Other rides at theme parks are modern versions of the standard rides seen at traditional amusement parks, as well as rides that Disney introduced, like the miniature turnpike automobiles (also produced by Arrow) or the monorail. There is always a tower at least 300 feet high that enables park visitors to view the whole affair at once as well as the surrounding city or countryside. There is music of all kinds, dance bands, vaudeville acts, circus acts, light melodramatic opera productions, and big name entertainment presented throughout the parks.

Astroworld, U.S.A., was the first major theme park to follow in Six Flags' footsteps. It was built in Houston by Roy M. Hofheinz, who decided to supplement his

Performing dolphins at Six Flags Over Mid-America.

"Eighth Wonder of the World," the Astrodome, with a theme park. The 57-acre park opened in 1968 just a stone's throw from the Astrodome, but since its opening it has been losing money. It is operating in the shadow of Six Flags Over Texas, and although the two theme parks are 200 miles apart, the Houston population and travelers seem content to drive to the Dallas park. Due to its several years of experience, Six Flags

This group is obviously having a great time on the "Zambezi Zinger," an ultramodern roller coaster at Worlds of Fun.

A portion of Astroworld, U.S.A., with the Astrodome in the distance.

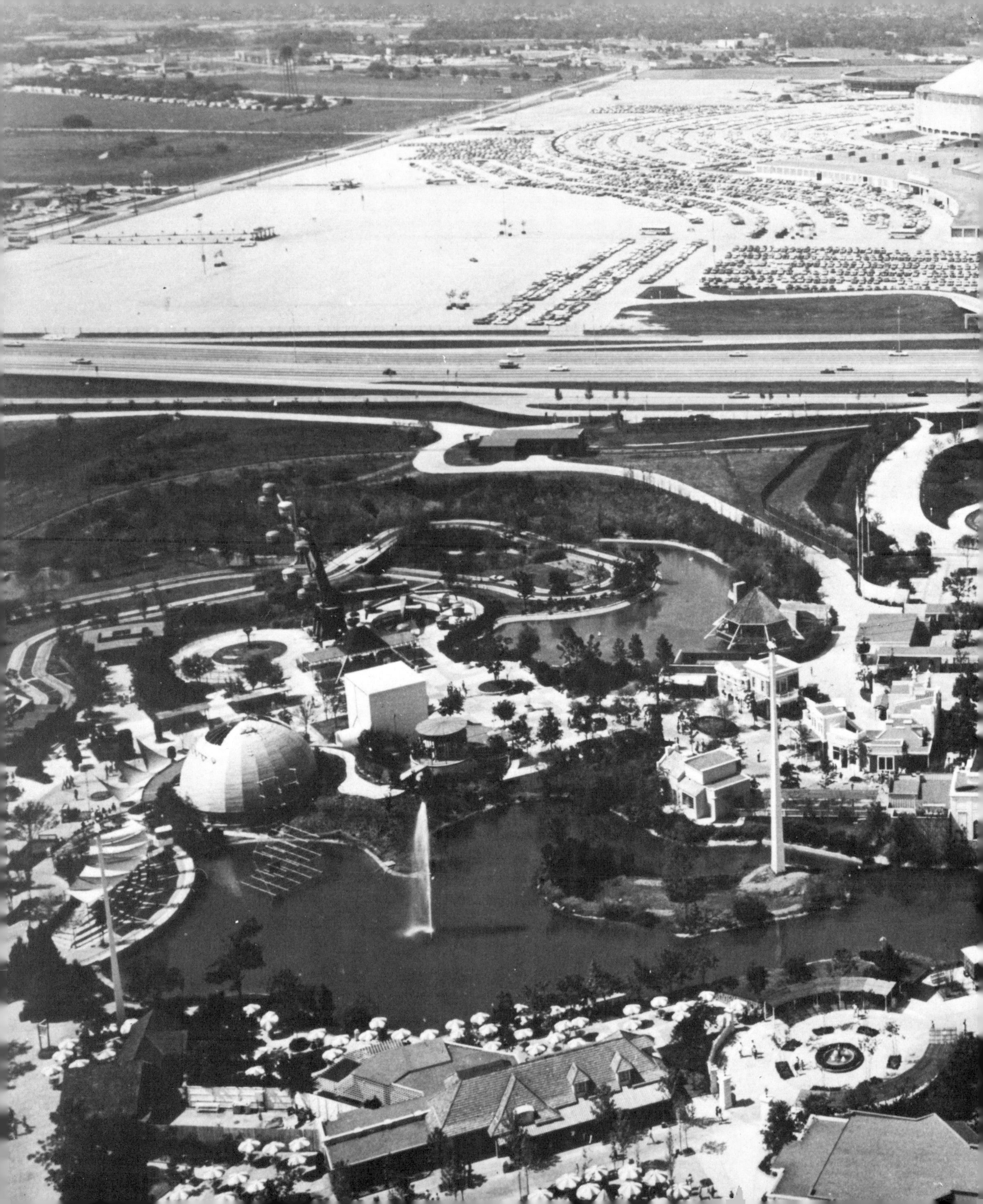

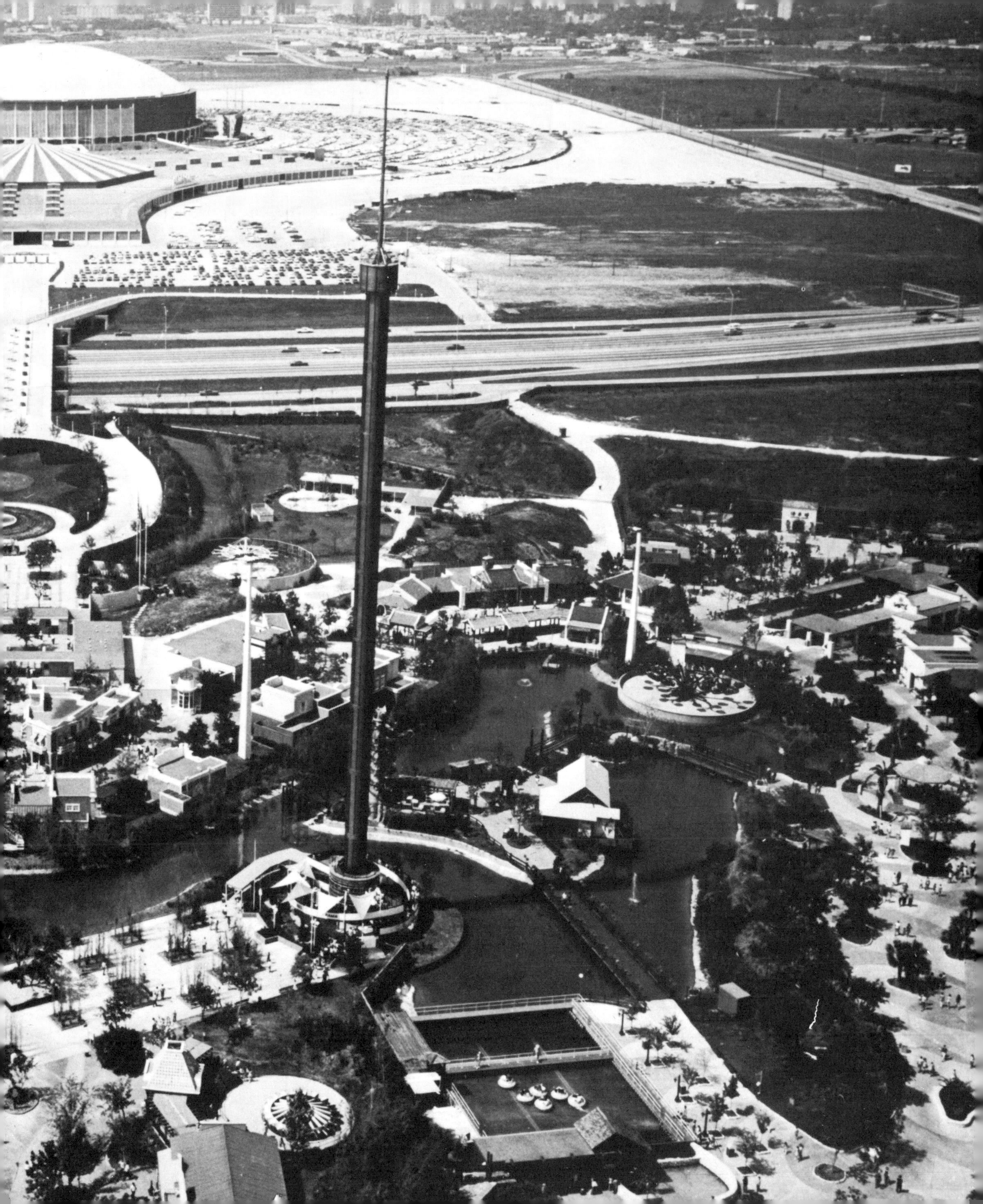

Marco Polo himself is the ambassador of fun at Marco Polo Park.

Over Texas displays a know-how in amusement park management that Astroworld obviously lacks. A major renovation in 1972 failed to put Astroworld on firmer ground, and in 1975 the park decided to sell itself to Six Flags, Inc., which hopes to use its expertise to make Astroworld a successful theme park.

Worlds of Fun was opened in Kansas City by sports tycoon Lamar Hunt in 1970. Like Astroworld, its size and capacity is less than most of the other major theme parks, but unlike Astroworld, it is enjoying success. It also appears a bit less superfluous than Astroworld. Whereas Astroworld's ten themed areas tend to confuse visitors, Worlds of Fun limited itself to four well-divided themes.

Marco Polo Park was built by Leisure and Recreation Concepts, Inc., just north of Daytona Beach, Florida. While smaller than Astroworld, U.S.A., Worlds of Fun, the park presents a more original and unified set of themes: the five explored worlds of Marco Polo: Turkey, India, China, Venice, and Japan. Marco Polo Park is a more relaxed theme park than the others, and yet it has a quiet attractiveness which pulled in a healthy 1,000,000-plus visitors in its first season in 1974.

Carowinds, opened the same year as Marco Polo Park, sits on the state line between North and South Carolina. Like Marco Polo Park, Carowinds makes up in beauty and atmosphere for what it may be lacking in thrills, and it, too, is doing quite well. Its theme—the history of the Carolinas—is less original, though, and it could as well have been called Six Flags Over Carolina.

A much more ambitious project than these four parks was opened in 1971 just north of Los Angeles by the Newhall Land and Farming Company and Sea World, Inc. It was called Magic Mountain, and in its first two years of operation it looked as if it would go the same route as the Denver park. "The park simply wasn't ready to open," recalls Terry VanGorder, Magic Mountain's general manager. "The premature opening meant a half-landscaped, dry-looking park, an inexperienced staff, and ride breakdowns. Generally the park was a giant bomb its opening season. We improved quickly, but the word of mouth killed us for the 1972 season." After two years of running in the red, Sea World sold itself out in a panic, deciding to concentrate on its own familiar territory of running sea-life parks.

Going it alone, the Newhall Company decided to try for one more season, and if it didn't pull itself into the black, Magic Mountain would have to close. But what would it take? The park had, since its poor opening, almost doubled its ride capacity, what had looked like a dry desert was now abounding in greenery, the food services had improved, and the staff was experienced and ready. The item they added was what most parks go to in order to secure crowds and help sell the park—name entertainment. It is expensive, but it usually works. Magic Mountain presented an impressive 1973 summer lineup of week-long shows which included Sonny and Cher, the Supremes, Bill Cosby, Phyllis Diller, Rich Little, and the Lennon Sisters.

The crowds poured into Magic Mountain that summer, and have been increasing phenomenally ever since. The park is now worth over $70,000,000, and while it still presents a summer lineup of name acts, visitors are coming more to enjoy the park itself.

Even more boldly impressive than Magic Mountain is the beautiful Kings Island,

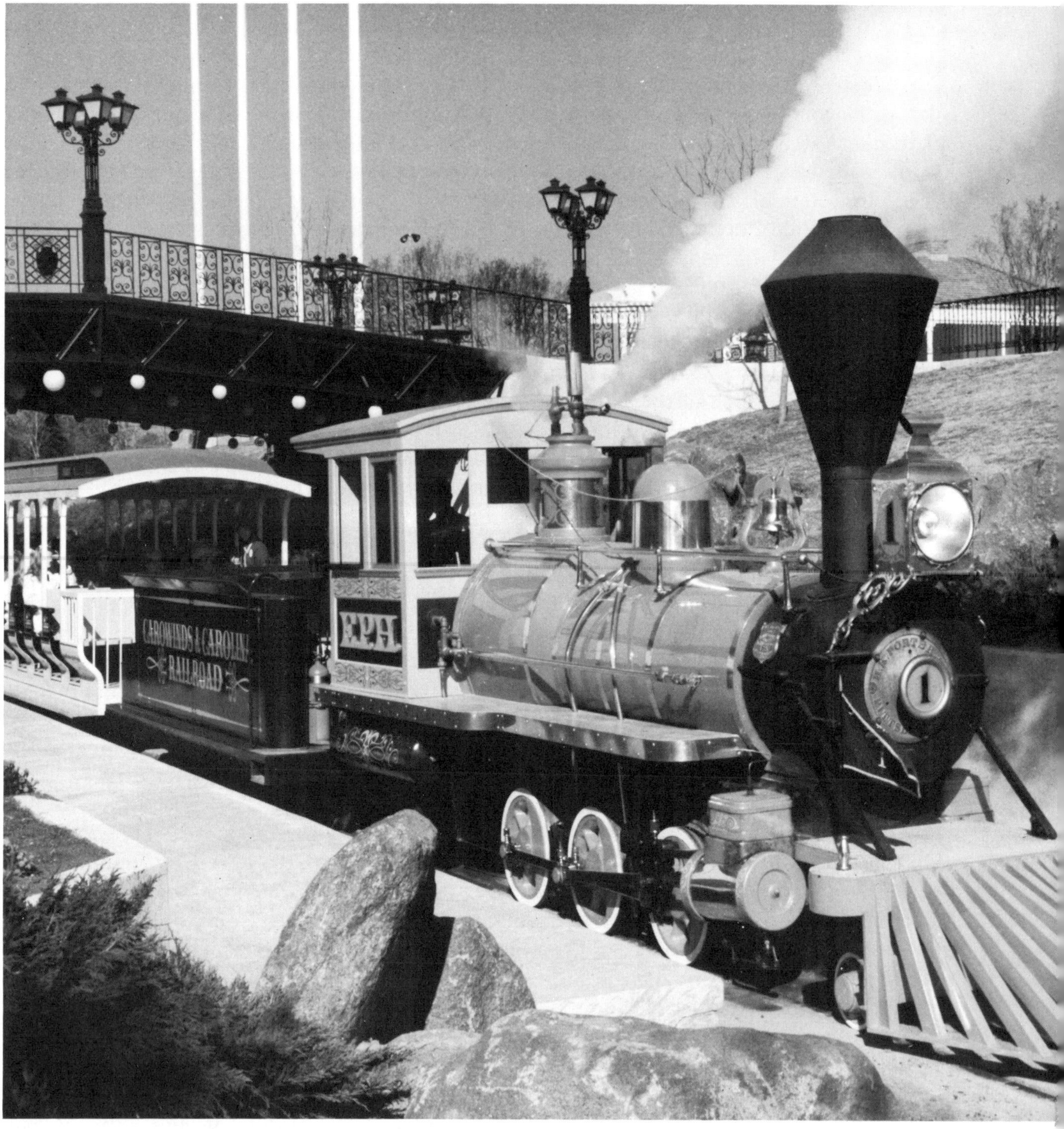
E.P.H.
RAILROAD

The Old Country.

The Carowinds and Carolina Railroad steams
back and forth across the Carolina border.

At Magic Mountain's petting zoo a baby elephant named Bamboo makes a friend.

which opened in 1972 just north of Cincinnati. It is owned and operated by the Taft Broadcasting Company, who were also the last owners of Cincinnati's Coney Island. Kings Island was being built in 1972 during Coney Island's last season as its new home that would be forever free from floods. One of Kings Island's five themed areas, all of which center around a striking one-third-scale replica of the Eiffel Tower, is appropriately named after Coney Island, and it contains a mall area similar to the original.

In 1975, in association with Top Value Enterprises, Taft also opened up Kings Dominion, a sister park in Richmond, Virginia. Its initial investment was $50,000,000, making it the third most costly amusement park investment, after Disney's two parks. Kings Dominion's format is similar to the Cincinnati park, and like that park, cartoon characters of the Hanna Barbera television shows (owned by Taft) roam through the park spreading cheer and acting as ambassadors of fun. The park helps out the TV shows, and the TV shows do their share of mentioning the park.

Many of the fine old carousels were bought and reconditioned at great expense by theme parks. This sixty-three-year-old beauty is at Magic Mountain in Los Angeles.

Another two-market theme park is the colorful Opryland, U.S.A. in Nashville, Tennessee. It houses the new home of the Grand Ole Opry, the famous radio show that started in 1925 as a showcase for American folk, country, and Western music. Opryland's theme is simply American music, and besides the Grand Ole Opry there are ten different musical shows presented throughout the park, not to mention the strolling minstrels and bands. There is only a limited number of rides, as Opryland insists on keeping the accent on its shows, proudly boasting that it is the only major theme park to present "the authenticity and uniqueness of America rather than its fantasy." Avoiding fantasy is a different way of presenting an amusement park, theme or traditional, but at Opryland, U.S.A. it works quite well.

If there is a non-Disney theme park to end all theme parks as far as size and scope it is probably Great Adventure in Jackson, New Jersey. It opened in 1974 on 1,500 acres of land, and is divided into the "Safari" and the "Enchanted Forest." The Safari is the

Magic Mountain's newest thriller is a head-over-heels loop roller coaster called the "Great American Revolution."

International Street, the Royal Fountain, and the Eiffel Tower at Kings Island.

Kings Island's Racer is a duplicate of Kings Dominion's Rebel Yell.

Music of all kinds abounds at Opryland, U.S.A.

largest drive-through safari park outside of Africa, with over 2,000 wild animals. The Enchanted Forest is the theme park, with the world's longest flume ride, the world's largest bumper car ride, the world's highest Ferris wheel, and every other type of ride imaginable. Three major live shows are presented throughout the park's three themed areas. The Aqua Spectacle is a 3,500-seat marine stadium with trained dolphins and Acapulco cliff divers performing off a 100-foot board. The band shell has two alternating bands providing continuous entertainment. And the show stopper is the 6,000-seat Great Arena, featuring circus and aerial acts, chariot races, jousting, and skydivers. What Coney Island's Dreamland was to the turn of the century, Great Aventure is to the present. There is no other word for it except sensational.

The idea of "chain" amusement parks started by Six Flags was taken a step further when the Marriott Corporation—one of the giants in worldwide restaurant and hotel operation—began building its three Great America parks. The two located in Chicago and Santa Clara, California, opened in 1976, and the third, in Washington, D.C., is scheduled to open in 1978. Not only is Marriott's impressive project unique in that two parks had a simultaneous opening (the Washington park was delayed due to zoning problems), but all three of the Great America parks are exactly the same, down to the very last detail. It seems the only difference is in the staff.

"We're dealing more with the regional patrons rather than the travelers," explains Bruce Burtch, the public-affairs manager of the Santa Clara park. "We don't expect people to have to drive halfway across the country to visit a Great America park, so we have made three identical parks. Ideally, we'd like to dot the entire nation with Great America parks, so we could bring to everybody what we feel the Marriott Corporation stands for—the very best in food and family entertainment."

The "very best" appears not to be an overstatement as evidenced by the $40,-000,000 Great America parks. While they have less capacity than the Taft parks or Great Adventure and lack the universal magical appeal of the Disney parks, the variety of entertainment—particularly the live shows—is superb, and they are certainly among the best planned and detail-perfect theme parks in the world.

"We're very concerned with keeping our five themed areas as authentic as possible," says Burtch. "Everything, including each plant, prop, food item, and piece of merchandise, is true to the specific era we're creating. Also, we want to avoid the problem many other theme parks have of their themed areas running into each other, or the visual intrusion of the outside world." To accomplish this Great America's five themed areas are well separated by shrubbery or other visual barriers. Guests traverse from one area to the other on covered bridges. A 20-foot-high embankment circling the park blocks out the surrounding city, keeping the fantasy mood intact.

Like many theme parks, Great America's attractions are built in a circular format in order to keep a smooth two-way flow of crowds. A well-hidden "artery road" leads from the employee parking lot into the center of the park, from where service and maintenance can be carried on out to the park's five areas, out of view of the park patrons. This "center core" type of operation is neat and efficient, and keeps theme-costumed workers from having to cross through a different themed area to get to their own. The Disney parks keep the service and maintenance hidden and the costumed

Acrobats in Great Adventure's Great Arena.

employees within their own areas by building an elaborate network of underground tunnels leading to the various park segments. Great America was able to find a much less expensive way of accomplishing the same task through their circular construction.

In addition to the major theme parks, there are approximately another one hundred parks in the United States which call themselves theme parks, although few of these have rides of any sort. These are the "attraction" parks. The first type of attraction parks were the "Old West" parks, with a cowboys, Indians, and Gold Rush theme. Knott's Berry Farm in Southern California was the first such park. While just a few miles away from Disneyland, Knott's Berry Farm didn't start out in Disney's footsteps as a theme park, as it had actually been a theme attraction since 1940. However, not until 1970 could it really be considered an amusement park of any sort.

The whole Walter Knott success story began in 1920 when he and his wife Corde-

*Chariot races are one of the star attractions
in Great Adventure's Great Arena.*

lia opened a roadside berry stand out of their 10-acre berry patch. Eight years later, the Knotts had a Berry Market, where they sold berry plants, and Mrs. Knott served berry pies in a small tearoom. In 1932, Walter Knott completed work begun by Rudolf Boysen on crossing a loganberry, blackberry, and red raspberry, resulting in a new fruit called the boysenberry.

The Knott's Berry Market became a well-known stopping place for travelers from Los Angeles on their way to the Newport Beach resort area, and business was increasing rapidly. In 1934, in order to create a higher income during the Depression, Mrs. Knott began serving chicken dinners in the tearoom. Her delicious fried chicken gained such a reputation in Southern California that the Knotts were able to open up a dining room on the farm.

From then on the farm's expansion was nonstop. In 1940, as a living memorial to

*Great America in Santa Clara is
shown here midway through construction.*

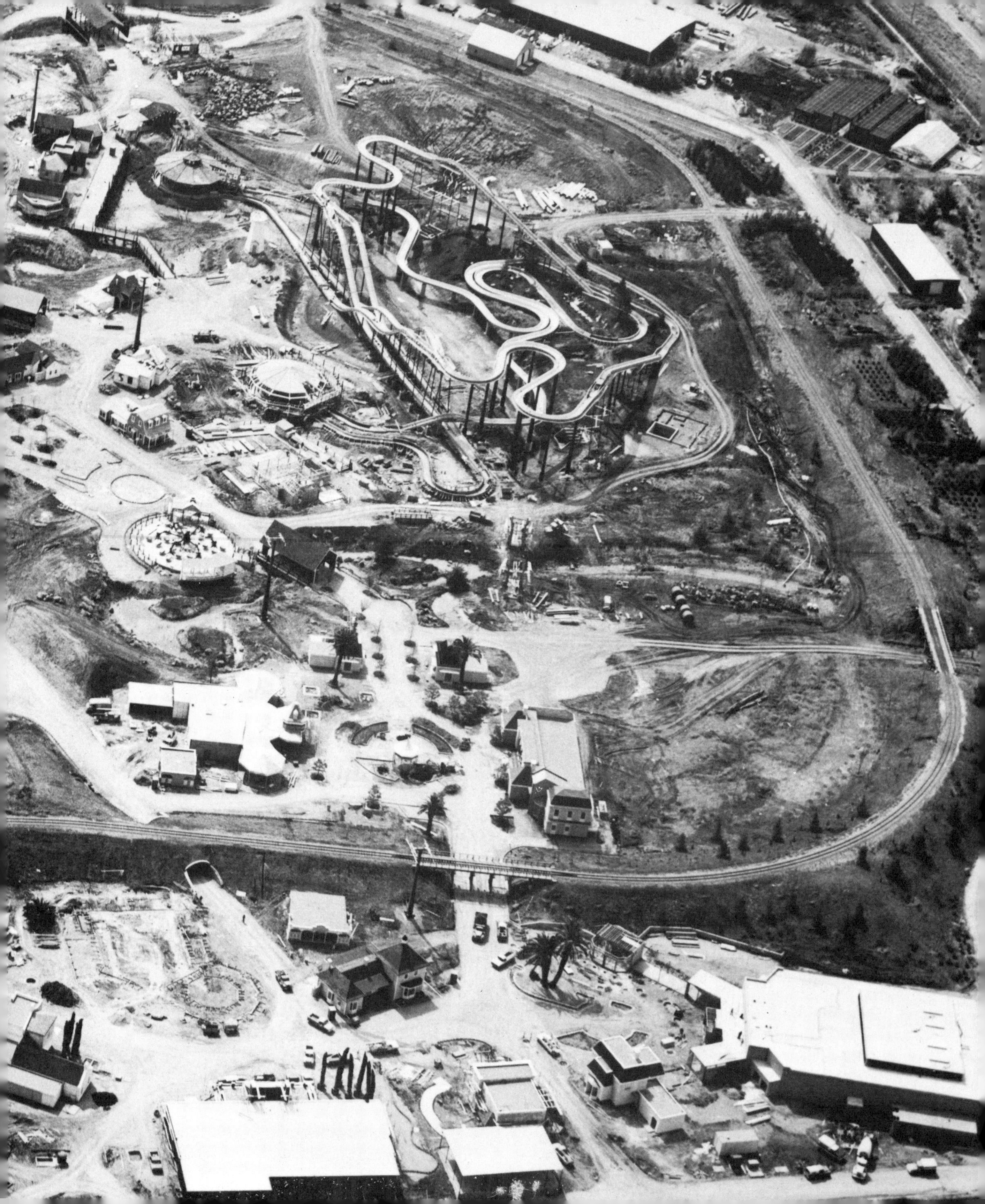

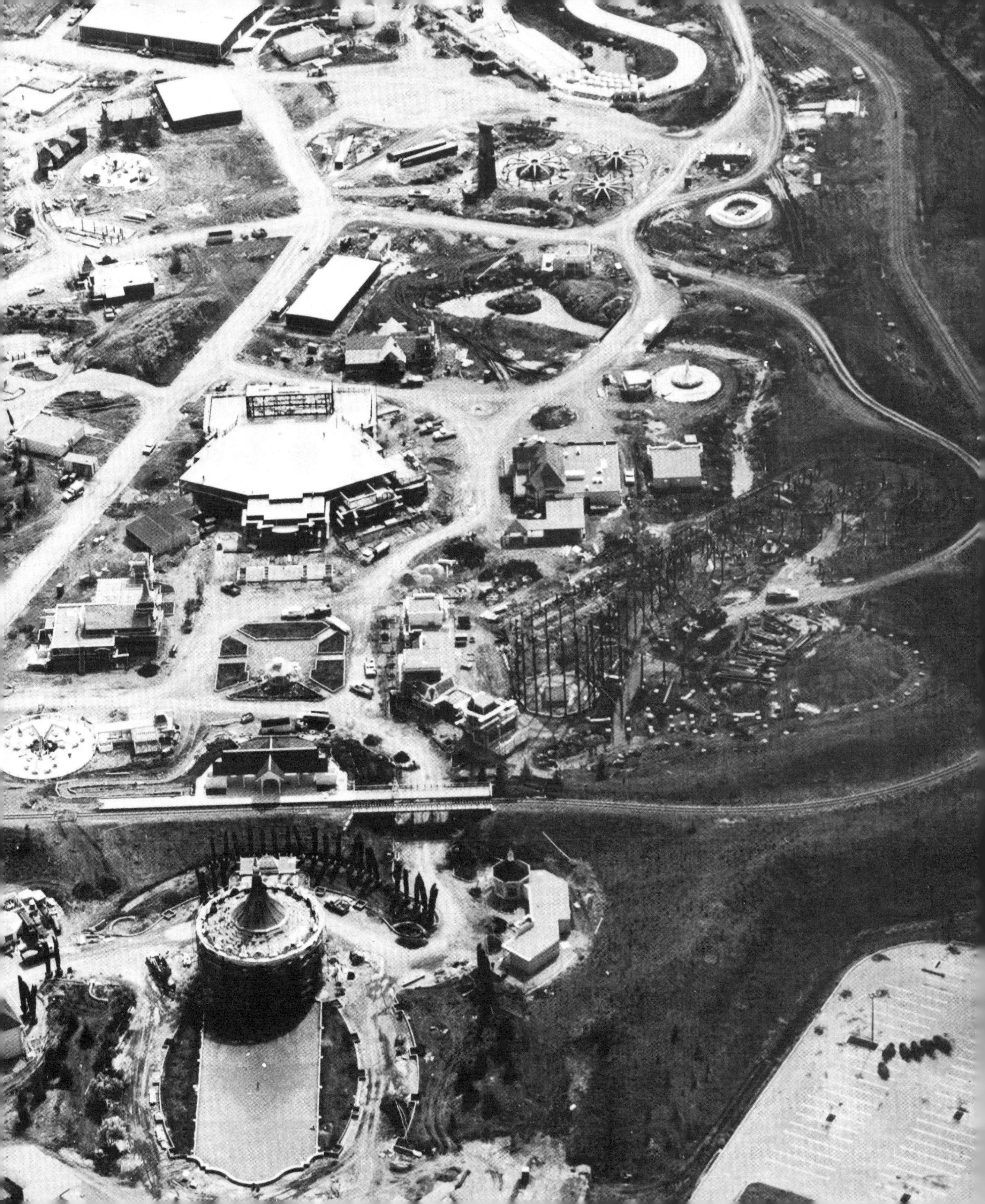

Workers prepare Great America for its 1976 opening.

Walter Knott's grandmother who had come west in a covered wagon, the Knotts began building the farm up in the spirited theme of the westward movement. They added an indoor historical presentation called the Covered Wagon show, and they built a realistic ghost town with buildings brought in, board for board, from various old deserted gold-rush towns. To the Ghost Town were added a stagecoach ride, a Western train ride, the "Calico Lost Mine Ride," the "Haunted Shack," and a Gold Mine where guests could really pan for gold.

In 1970, several thrill rides were added, turning Knott's Berry Farm into a full-fledged theme amusement park, its three themes being the original Old West Ghost Town, Fiesta Village—depicting early California—and the Roaring Twenties—an amusement park of the 1920s. The Knott's youngest daughter, Marion Knott Anderson, continues the family tradition of improving and expanding Knott's Berry Farm, making it one of the nation's finest theme parks.

The early American beer gardens enjoyed a thematic reawakening of sorts when in 1959 the Anheuser-Busch Corporation, brewers since 1860, opened up a new type of attraction park in Tampa, Florida. Busch Gardens is a beautifully landscaped park full of lakes, waterfalls, gardens, and exotic birds. Its original forte was simply a pleasant atmosphere where complimentary Busch and Michelob beer was served, and the brewery could be toured.

The idea for Busch Gardens had come from the private gardens created in 1903 by Adolphus Busch, one of the original partners, and his wife in Pasadena, California. Like Elitch's Gardens in Denver, the original 30-acre Busch Gardens were eventually opened to the public, who came from all over Southern California to stroll through the gardens,

Kings Dominion.

enjoying flower beds, palm trees, statues, and ponds. But no amusements of any kind were added, and the gardens were closed in 1928 following the deaths of Mr. and Mrs. Busch.

A few years after its opening the Tampa Busch Gardens expanded to feature an African theme, with over 800 African wild animals in natural habitats viewed from a Monorail Safari. In contrast, the second Busch Gardens park opened in 1966 in Los Angeles with a tropical theme, featuring a walk-through bird aviary and a trained bird show. Like the Tampa park, this Busch Gardens had no admission charge until theme rides were later added, when a pay-one-price admission policy was established.

The third Busch park, The Old Country, was opened in Williamsburg, Virginia, in 1975. More on the line of a standard theme park than the other two parks, The Old Country is split into Germany, France, and England, and cleverly advertises itself as "Europe for $6.50." Like the other two Busch parks, there are only a few rides, but the three areas are high in authenticity, offering shops, restaurants and entertainment that makes The Old Country, along with Great America and the Disney parks, thematically one of the finest parks in the nation.

It was over half a century before the world's first amusement park, Paul Boyton's Sea Lion Park, was to be thematically revived. In 1954, Marineland of the Pacific was the first of the many sea life attractions parks. Located on a bluff overlooking the Pacific in Southern California, Marineland presents an amazing and highly entertaining series of aquatic shows, featuring performing dolphins, killer whales, sea lions, pearl divers, and 100-foot high-divers. There are several large and beautiful aquariums with hundreds of varieties of fish. Walruses, penguins, and the very rare elephant seals

The Ghost Town in Knott's Berry Farm.

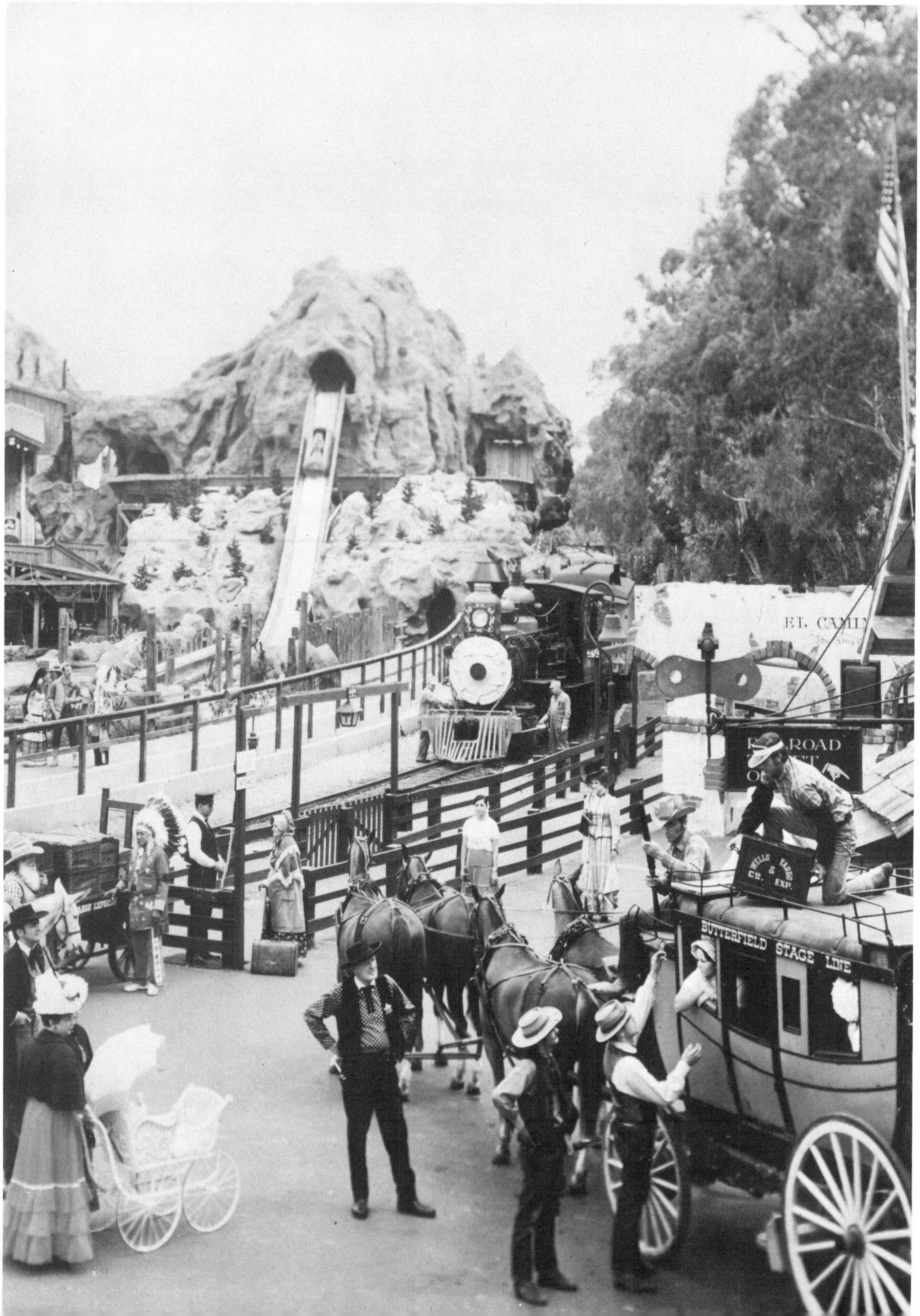
BUTTERFIELD STAGE LINE

The Corkscrew in the Roaring 20's section of Knott's Berry Farm.

Busch Gardens in Tampa.

can be viewed in well-simulated habitats. In short, Marineland of the Pacific made it possible for people to experience oceanic life in as near to a natural environment as possible, providing a fascinating and fun-filled day. With its success, several sea-life parks have opened across the nation, the most successful of which is Sea World, Inc., with parks in San Diego, California; Aurora, Ohio; and Orlando, Florida.

As popular and in the same vein as the Sea-Life parks are the wild animal or safari parks, most of which are owned by Lion Country Safari, Inc. This company was started by Harry Shuster, who realized that the many popular drive-through big game parks in Africa could conceivably be brought over to the snowfall-free parts of the United States. In 1967 he opened the first Lion Country Safari on 640 acres in the Florida Everglades. Visitors are able to drive their own cars or ride buses through the park, enjoying a first-rate view of a huge variety of wild animals. What everyone— particularly zoologists—notices is that the animals look, act, and in fact feel healthier and happier than those animals seen in the oppressive cages of a zoo. As one editorial writer put it: "Lion Country Safari is the greatest thing to happen to endangered species of African wildlife since Noah's Ark."

Subsequent Lion Country Safaris were built in Los Angeles, California; Stockbridge, Georgia; and Grand Prairie, Texas; and two others became integral parts of Taft's Kings Island and Kings Dominion parks. They all receive worldwide zoological praise for the care and conservation of the animals, particularly several endangered species.

Two rather unusual theme attraction parks that have received a good amount of publicity, and controversy, opened in 1975. One is Holyland in Mobile, Alabama; the other is Bible World, in Orlando, Florida. The two parks contain such attractions as paintings and murals depicting stories from the Old and New Testaments, a Jerusalem marketplace, a Tower of Babel slide, a Garden of Eden, and animated speaking Biblical figures which relate the story of the birth of Jesus Christ. Somehow the word "amusement" or even "park," seems blasphemous in such a setting.

George Tilyou's indoor 5-acre Pavilion of Fun now seems quite small when compared to Old Chicago, a 57-acre enclosed combination amusement park and shopping center. It was opened in Chicago in 1975 and contains 31 rides and attractions and over 200 retail stores and eating places. Built by Recreational Retail Builders, Inc., at a cost of $40,000,000, Old Chicago is the world's first major amusement park which can be in full operation regardless of the weather. The 586,000-square-foot building is climate-controlled, enabling it to operate on a year-round basis.

The ride area is in the center of the huge domed building, containing games,

Busch Gardens in Los Angeles.

Oktoberfest in the German burg of The Old Country.

Shakespeare's Globe Theater in The Old Country presents an elaborate Shakespearean production.

Lion Country Safari.

circus acts, musical variety shows, and over 20 major rides. Its theme is the Old Chicago Fairgrounds after the World's Columbian Exposition, although it is actually more in line with a traditional amusement park than a theme park. Yet it is still one of the unique amusement parks in history, and to see full-sized Ferris wheels and roller coasters operating indoors is rather awesome.

Out of the over 800 permanent parks now in operation in the United States, about 450 are attraction parks. Another 150 are either picnic grounds with a few rides on the side, or "kiddielands." The rest are major theme and traditional amusement parks.

Kiddielands are tiny amusement parks with about 15 miniature rides for the six-and-under set. They became big in the 1950s, and for a while almost every city with a population of at least 50,000 had one. They were usually near a shopping center in order to get business from mothers who have taken their small children shopping with them. A whining child was almost sure to drag his tired mother over to the kiddieland.

There are considerably fewer kiddielands around today, as most major theme parks contain an elaborate section for small children. But there are a lot of "Fairyland"

Lion Country Safari at Kings Dominion.

parks. These are children's parks in a dreamy, usually woodsy setting, with fairy tales or folklore as the theme. The many "Santa Claus Land" attraction parks serve as fitting examples, with their candy houses, sleigh rides, the North Pole, and old Saint Nick himself.

Out of the remaining 200 major amusement parks, only about 30 are theme parks, but they draw over 50 percent of the revenue. Theme parks are so successful because they draw in the families more than the traditional amusement parks do, thanks to their clean, lovely settings and their abundance of family entertainment. Also, they collect an average of $5.00 per person at the gate (children under three are admitted free at almost all theme parks), so a larger profit is made than if prices were charged per ride or per show. At traditional parks with a pay-as-you-ride policy, most adults merely walk around the park letting their children enjoy the rides and attractions, rather than pay extra money to enjoy everything with their children. The pay-one-price policy is much more profitable for the park, convenient for the patron, and it keeps the family together.

The indoor amusement park of Old Chicago.

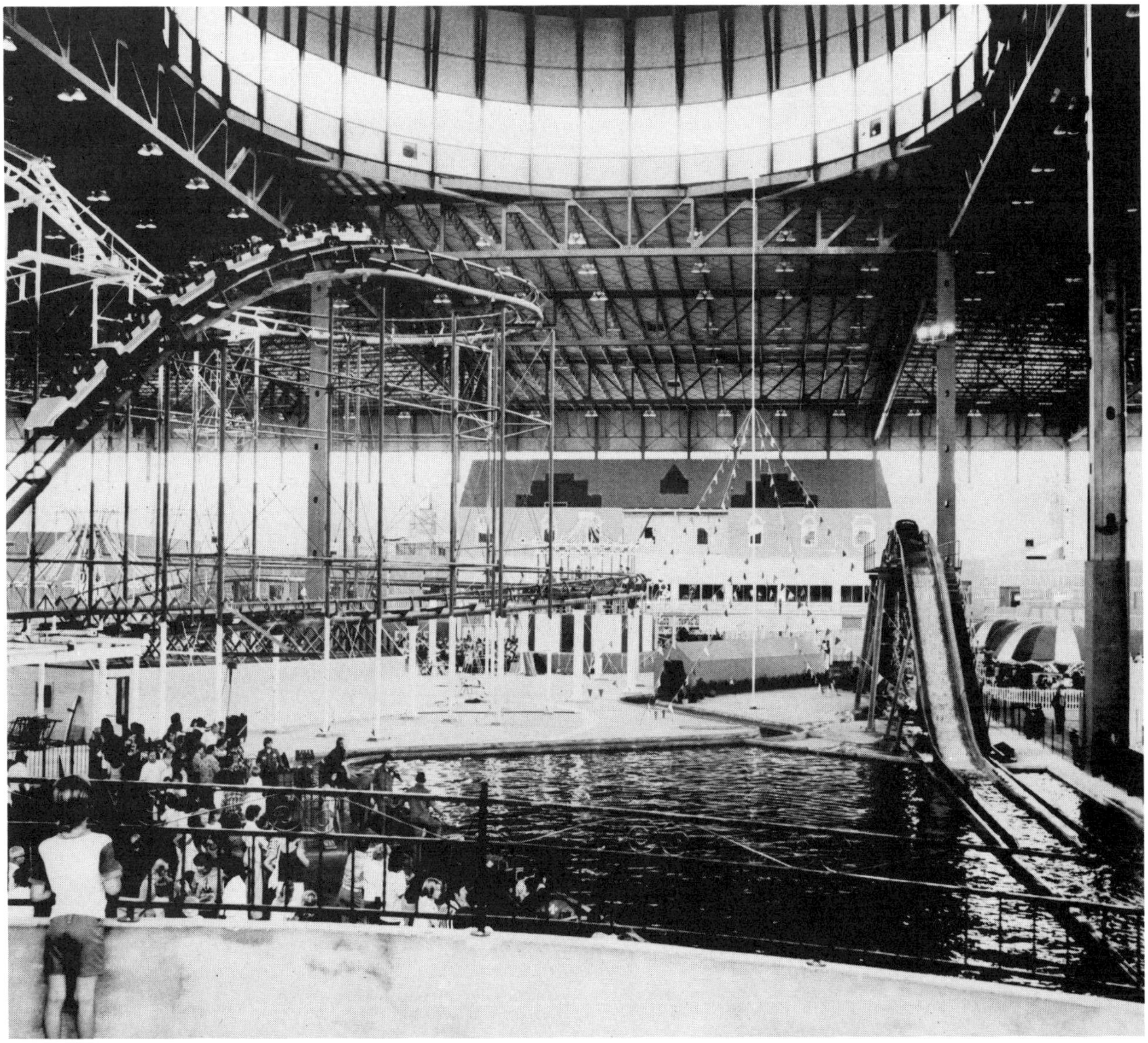

Old Chicago.

Walt Disney World. (© Walt Disney Productions)

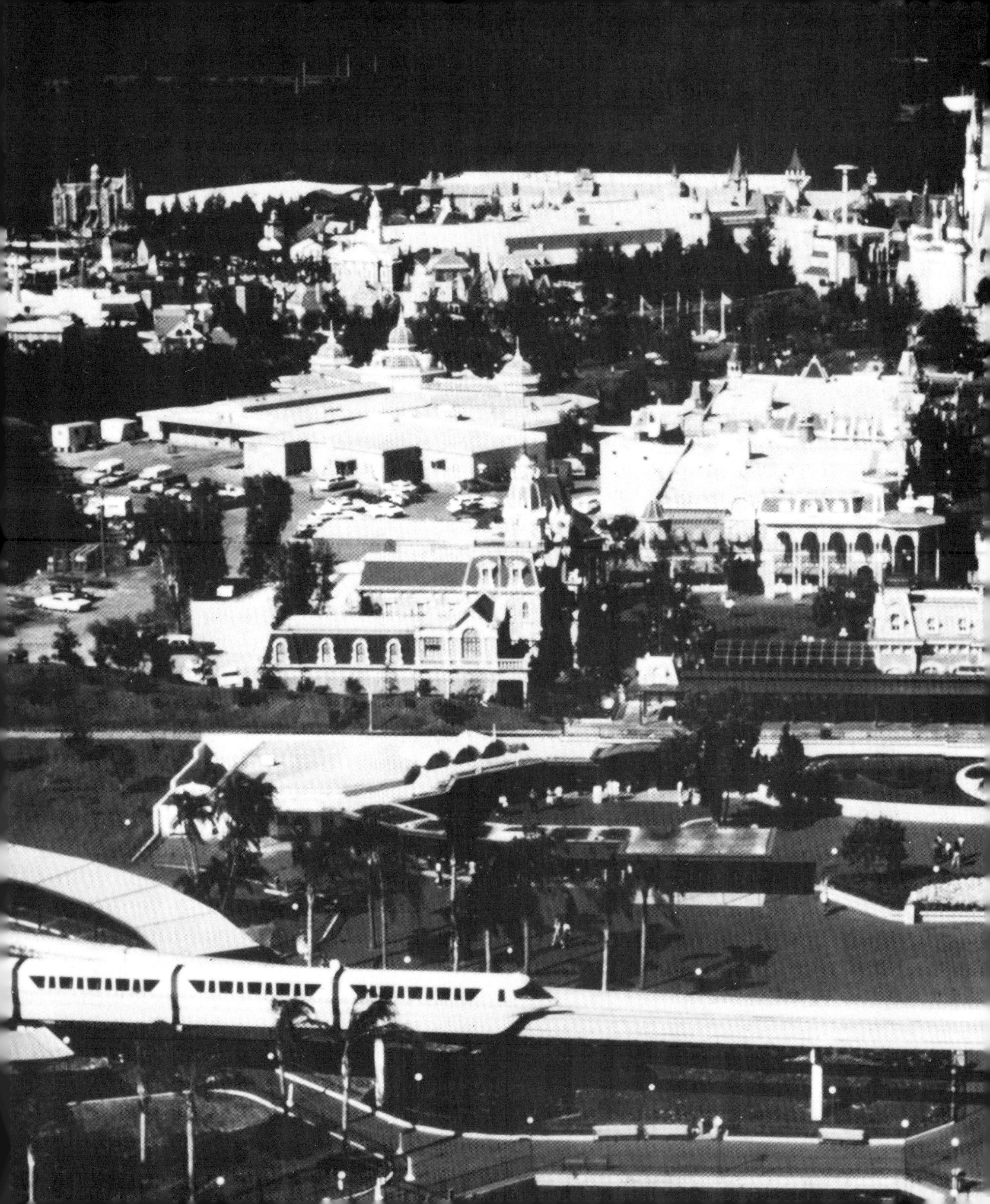

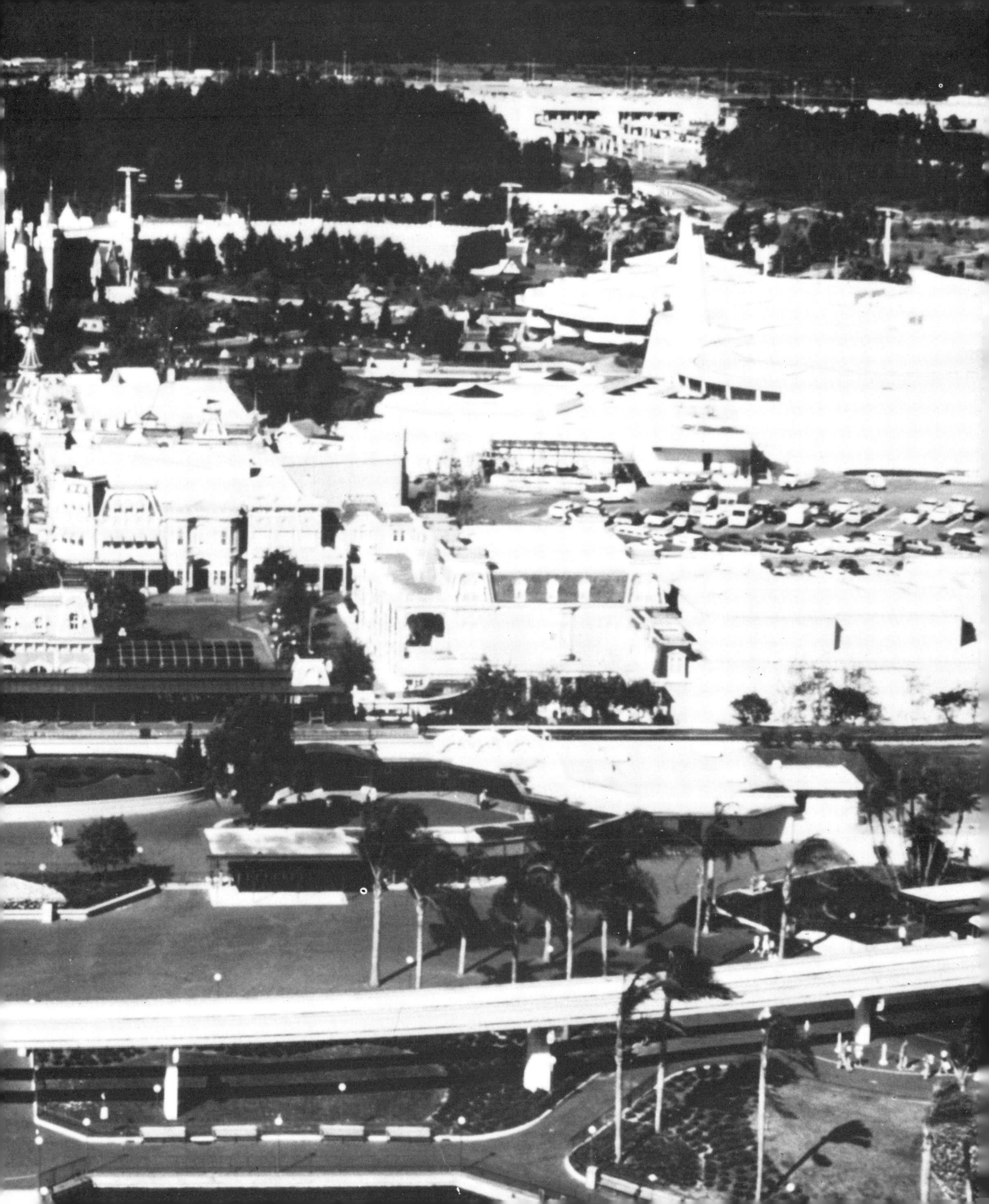

The eighteen-story Cinderella Castle in Walt Disney World's Magic Kingdom. (© Walt Disney Productions)

In the meantime, the original theme park, Disneyland, was to be joined by a sister park in 1965 when Walt Disney announced his plans to open Walt Disney World (originally named Disneyland East) in Florida, 55 miles west of Cape Kennedy at Orlando. Since Disneyland's opening in 1955, Disney had been dismayed at the fast growth of motels, restaurants, freeways, and service stations which had mushroomed around the park, and by 1958 held it in a choked-in environment. Walt Disney World, as he announced, would encompass a total of 27,400 acres, so that the environment could be controlled. While the Magic Kingdom theme park of Walt Disney World would be approximately the same size and basic plan of Disneyland, Disney wanted to surround the park with his own environmentally clean and controlled area, thereby curtailing commercial development.

In October of 1971, the $100,000,000 Walt Disney World opened, by far the largest, most beautiful, and most spectacular man-made vacation resort in the world. For the 10,000,000 people who visit it each year, Walt Disney World has three resort hotels—the Contemporary, the Golf Resort, and the Polynesian Village—and extensive and roomy camping at Fort Wilderness Campland. Guests reach the Magic Kingdom by way of

Captain Nemo's Nautilus Submarine takes Walt Disney World visitors underwater and down to the "ocean floor." (© Walt Disney Productions)

steamboat or monorail. There are two golf courses, and boating and water skiing are available on the large clean lakes. In short, Walt Disney World is a dreamland of vacationing, and it still covers only one-tenth of all its acreage. What will be done with the rest of the land is limited only by the imagination. Walt Disney Productions is now planning the building of a modern, environmentally clean and safe city somewhere within the area.

The fantasy, magic, nostalgia, and Americana of Walt Disney's many creations had begun to be harshly criticized in the early 1950s, as art critics bitterly denied Disney any artistic merit, labeling his animated films as no more than "bawdy cartoons, full of racist and vulgar insinuations." Disneyland was referred to by many as an "amusement park supermarket" and Disney himself was criticized for his American conservatism.

But Walt Disney was undaunted by the intellectual attack which was constantly upon him. Shortly before his death on December 15, 1966, he said, "What I do was never supposed to be considered art. This is show business, and I'm a showman." George Tilyou couldn't have said it better.

The 86 characters of the Mickey Mouse Revue are another Audio-Animatronics feature at Walt Disney World. (© Walt Disney Productions)

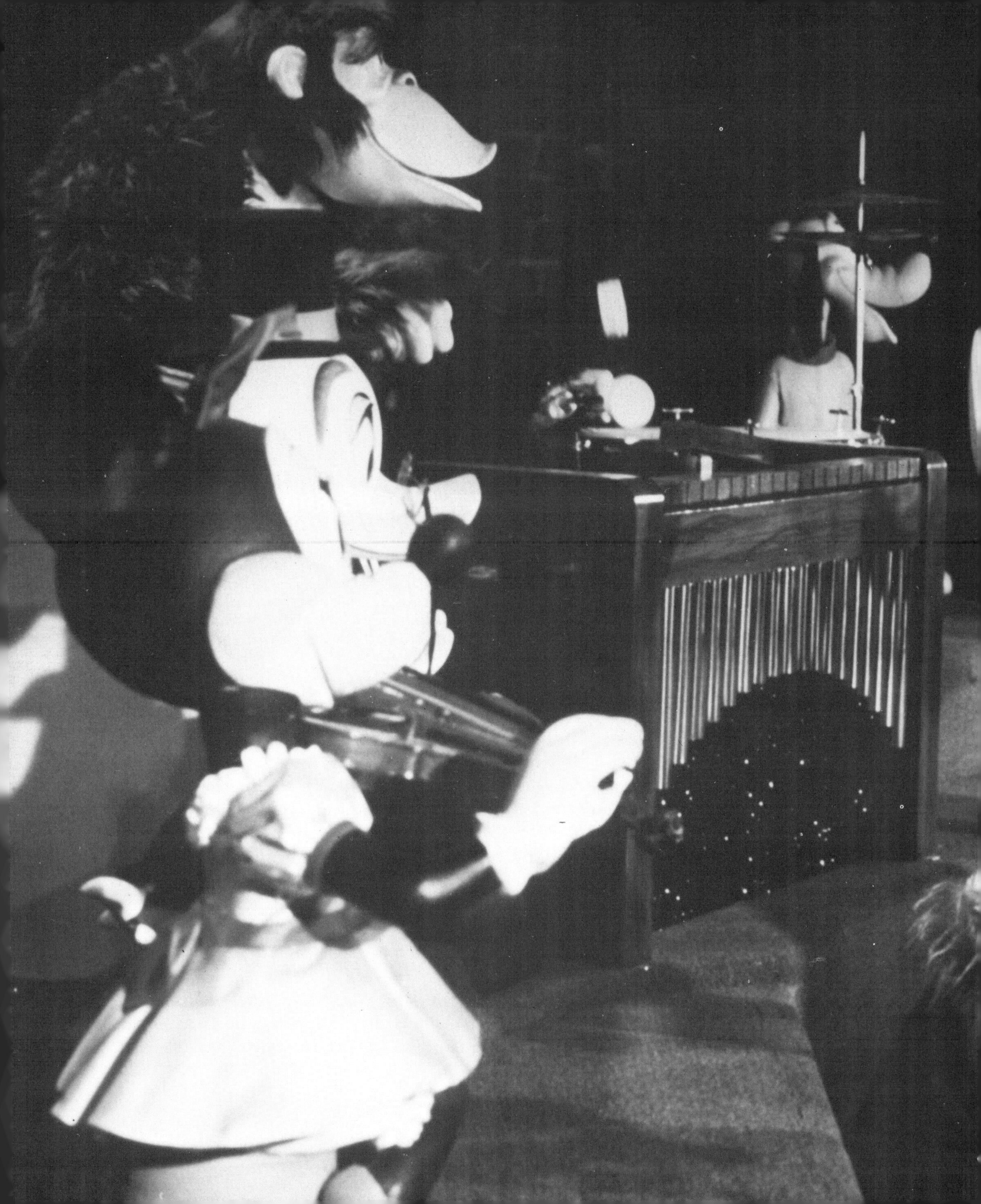

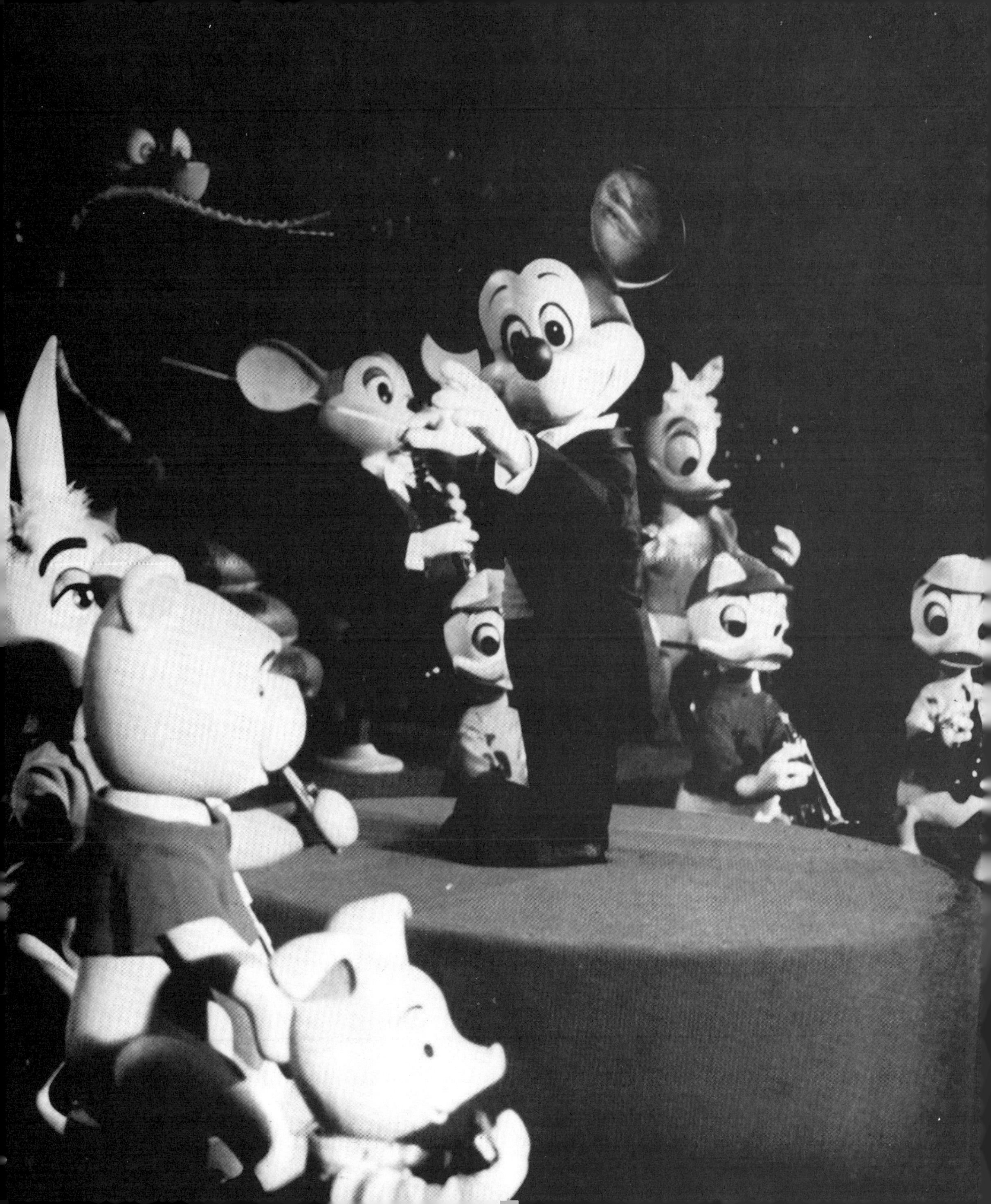

Chapter Six
America's Top 100 Parks

LISTED HERE are the 100 best of America's theme amusement parks, traditional amusement parks, and attraction parks today in operation. The parks can be written to or called for brochures or information. Prices and operating hours are not listed here, as they change often.

Big Surf.

ARIZONA

BIG SURF; 1500 North Hayden Road,
Tempe, Arizona 85281. (602)947–
2477

Located just outside of Phoenix, Big Surf is one of the most unusual attraction parks: it has the world's largest man-made ocean, complete with surf, right in the middle of the Arizona desert! Besides the surfing, body surfing, and rubber raft riding in the "ocean," there is a 300-foot-long "Surf Slide," which is like riding in the log flume ride, but without the log. There is a large beach complete with palm trees, plenty of refreshments, dancing, and big-name acts. Surfboards and rubber rafts can be rented.

The surf slide at Big Surf.

Frontier Village.

The Giant Dipper at Santa Cruz Beach and Boardwalk.

ARKANSAS

DOGPATCH, U.S.A.; Dogpatch, Arkansas 72648. (501)365-5483

Dogpatch, U.S.A., is the home of Li'l Abner, Daisy Mae, and the whole Al Capp comic strip gang, right in the middle of the Ozark Mountains. There are rides, plenty of musical entertainment, the Dogpatch Caverns, trout fishing, horseback riding, trained sea lions, and more. Located just south of Harrison on Highway 7, Dogpatch is open from the first weekened in May to the last weekend in October.

CALIFORNIA

FRONTIER VILLAGE; 4885 Monterey Road, San Jose, Ca. 95111. (408)225-1500

Frontier Village is one of the earliest of the Old West theme parks, complete with shootouts, stagecoach rides, train robberies, thrill rides, shows, an Old West Museum, games, and lots of family fun.

GREAT AMERICA; P.O. Box 1776, Santa Clara, Ca. 95052. (408) 988-1776

Like the other two Great America parks, this one is divided into Yankee Harbor, Yukon Territory, Great Midwest Livestock Exposition and County Fair, Hometown Square, and Orleans Place. Great America is located in Santa Clara, 45 miles south of San Francisco off U.S. 101.

Marineland of the Pacific.

Magic Mountain.

MARINE WORLD; Marine World Parkway, Redwood City, Ca. 94065. (415)591–7676

One of the newest of the sealife parks, Marine World runs the gamut from performing sea animals to a safari raft ride in the "Africa, U.S.A." section of the park. Like all of the California parks, Marine World is open year-round.

SANTA CRUZ BEACH AND BOARDWALK; Santa Cruz, Ca. 95060. (408)423–5590

Without doubt, Santa Cruz Beach and Boardwalk is the best and most beautiful seaside amusement park in the nation. Located on the northern shore of the Monterey Bay, Santa Cruz has everything a traditional amusement park should have, all topped by an entertaining indoor attraction called the "Cave Train." The large variety of food available is the best found in any park, and the bay offers good swimming.

Busch Gardens in Southern California.

MARINELAND OF THE PACIFIC; Palos Verdes, Ca. 90274. (213)772–1188

Not only is Marineland the first of the sea-life parks, it is still the best of them all, with the world's largest collection of marine mammals and fish, astounding shows, and a fun-filled Jungle Island. Marineland has the original killer whales, along with TV's Flipper.

MAGIC MOUNTAIN; 26101 Magic Mountain Parkway, Valencia, Ca. 91355. (805)259–7272

Located 25 miles north of Los Angeles on Interstate 5, Magic Mountain is one of the dozen "biggies" of the theme parks. Built around a moun-tain-perched 385-foot Sky Tower, the park has loads of exciting rides, a petting zoo, old-time movies, some delicious restaurants, and dancing under the stars. The biggest names in show business perform in the 3,400-seat Showcase Theater.

BUSCH GARDENS; 16000 Roscoe Blvd., Van Nuys, Ca. 91406. (213)997–1171

Within the lovely Busch Gardens is a boatride, a flume ride, animal shows, live acts, and free beer to adults over twenty-one. A monorail takes visitors through the brewery and gives them a bird's-eye view of the whole park. There are bumper cars and a fun house in the Old St. Louis section.

DISNEYLAND; 1313 Harbor Blvd., Anaheim, Ca. 92803. (714)533-4456

Disneyland is still the king of the theme parks, and really is a place everyone should visit. The Magic Kingdom has nonstop fun and entertainment, with acts and music of all kinds. New rides and shows are added each year since, as Disney said, Disneyland will never be complete.

UNIVERSAL CITY STUDIO TOURS; 100 Universal City Plaza, Universal City, Ca. 91608. (213)985-4321

This unique attraction park offers visitors an exciting and unforgettable behind-the-scenes look at Universal Studios, one of the world's largest producers in the television and motion picture industry. Here you can look at costumes, sets, and scenes from world-famous movies and watch stuntmen put on a thrilling barroom brawl and gunfight in a Western town. The headlining attraction of Universal City is a tram tour which takes you through the back lots of Universal, where you can see acres of outdoor sets used in television and movies and watch different Universal television series being filmed. The tram takes its riders through several special effects "catastrophes," including an avalanche, a runaway train, a collapsing bridge, and right through a parting of the Red Sea. Television and film stars are usually on hand for autographs to round out an exciting day.

LION COUNTRY SAFARI; 8800 Moulton Parkway, Laguna Hills, Ca. 92653. (714)837-1200

This is the second of the magnificent Lion Country Safari parks, located 70 miles south of Los Angeles on Interstate 5.

Lion Country Safari in Southern California.

KNOTT'S BERRY FARM; 8039 Beach Blvd., Buena Park, Ca. 90620. (714)827-1776

Knott's Berry Farm still serves its famous chicken dinners, along with a rich setting of old pioneer, Indian, and Spanish-American lore. The realistic Western Ghost Town is like a large museum piece, and name acts are presented in the Good Time Theater in the Roaring Twenties section. Located just a few miles from Disneyland, Knott's Berry Farm is open every day of the year.

BELMONT AMUSEMENT PARK; 3000 Mission Blvd., San Diego, Ca. 92109. (714)488-0531

Belmont Park is a traditional seaside amusement park that started in 1923 as Mission Beach Amusement Park.

A performing porpoise at Sea World of San Diego.

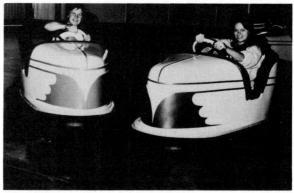

The Wheeler Dealer Bumper Cars in Knott's Berry Farm.

It is still playing host to large, enthused crowds, and is very well kept up, with over 30 rides, several games, and free shows.

SEA WORLD OF SAN DIEGO; 1720 South Shores Road, San Diego, Ca. 92109. (714)222-6363

Sea World of San Diego is the first of the Sea World, Inc., chain of parks. It offers fantastic marine shows and a sky tower offering a spectacular view of beautiful San Diego. Exotic foods are served in the various restaurants, and an exciting ride can be enjoyed on a high-speed hydrofoil.

COLORADO

ELITCH'S GARDENS; 4620 West 38th Ave., Denver, Col. 80012. (303)455-4771

For decades now, Elitch's Gardens has been the perfect combination of beautiful gardens and thrilling rides. The famous Elitch Theater still presents smash Broadway plays with big stars year round, and the Trocadero still presents the best in big-band music. "Mr. Twister" is among the best roller coasters in the nation.

LAKESIDE AMUSEMENT PARK;
4601 Sheridan Boulevard, Denver, Col. 80212. (313)477-1621

A more traditional amusement park than the neighboring Elitch's Gardens, Lakeside is amazing in the way it has so well preserved its beautiful buildings, walkways, and fountains from when the park opened at the turn of the century. The park has over 42 rides, including boatrides on the lake, one of the world's longest miniature train rides around the lake, and one of the few honest-to-goodness fun houses in the nation, beautifully intact and full of gags. This amusement park is a must-visit for anyone in Denver.

CONNECTICUT

LAKE COMPOUNCE; Bristol, Conn. 06010. (203)582-6333

Lake Compounce holds the distinction of being the nation's oldest amusement park in continuous operation under the same management. It was organized as a summer resort in 1846 and was turned into an amusement park after the turn of the century. It is still a popular resort, with the lake offering various water sports, and the park offering the various rides.

FLORIDA

RINGLING BROS.-BARNUM & BAILEY CIRCUS WORLD;
Barnum City, Fla. 32801. (305)841-6200

Florida is and always has been the winter home of the circus world, where new acts are prepared and old acts are kept in shape for the spring and summer circuit. Circus World is a theme attraction that takes you not only to but actually into the world of clowns, acrobats, and daredevils. The star attraction is the world's largest movie screen, which presents a breathtaking close-up view of a Ringling Bros.-Barnum & Bailey big top performance.

MARCO POLO PARK; Bunnell, Fla. 32018. (904)672-3220

This picturesque and pleasant theme park is located on Interstate 95, north of Daytona Beach.

PIRATES WORLD; 613 East Sheridan Street, Dania, Fla. 33004. (305)920-7800

Pirates World is somewhat weak on a unified theme, but there are plenty of rides and fun, including the famous Steeplechase Ride.

Lake Compounce.

*The Giant Wheel in Marco
Polo Park.*

*Walt Disney World. © Walt
Disney Productions)*

MARINELAND OF FLORIDA; St. Augustine, Fla. 32084. (904)829-5607

This sealife park is not connected with Marineland of the Pacific in California, but it provides the same excellent shows, aquariums, and entertainment.

WALT DISNEY WORLD; Lake Buena Vista, Fla. 32830. (305)824-2222

Currently the world's largest theme park, Walt Disney World has surpassed its toughest competitor, Disneyland, in everything except the nostalgic originality. It will be interesting to see what is done with all of the Disney-owned acreage surrounding the park in the upcoming years.

MIRACLE STRIP AMUSEMENT PARK; 12001 West Highway 98, Panama City, Fla. 32401. (904)234-3333

On any summer evening, Panama City Beach is the place for excitement, and most of it is harbored at Miracle Strip. Its fun-packed midway has over 30 rides, the star attraction being the "Old House," which is the cleverest walk-through haunted house in the nation. Miracle Strip is a superb example of the magical fun found at only the best traditional amusement parks.

PETTICOAT JUNCTION AMUSEMENT PARK; Long Beach Resort, Panama City, Fla. 32401. (904)234-2563

Named after the old television comedy show, Petticoat Junction is just one mile east of Miracle Strip. It contains the Cannonball No. 9 train, a deer ranch, an 1880s Western town, and plenty of rides.

BUSCH GARDENS; 3000 Busch Boulevard, Tampa, Fla. 33612. (813)988-8360

This is the first of the three Busch Gardens parks, with over 600 wild African animals, a Moroccan village, and an Old St. Louis section.

LION COUNTRY SAFARI; P.O. Box 16066, West Palm Beach, Fla. 33406. (305)793-1084

This is the original Lion County Safari park, located 17 miles west of Palm Beach.

GEORGIA

SIX FLAGS OVER GEORGIA; Interstate 20, Atlanta, Ga. 30336. (404)948-9290

This is the second of the Six Flags parks, set in a thick woodsy area across the Chattahoochee River from Atlanta. It is bright, colorful, and full of fun, presenting great shows in the Crystal Pistol and Sid and Marty Krofft's Puppet Theater and thrilling rides, all topped by the "Great American Scream Machine," and a 225 foot-high revival of the Parachute Jump.

Six Flags Over Georgia's "Great American Scream Machine."

THE WORLD OF SID AND MARTY KROFFT; 400 North-Omni International, Atlanta, Ga. 30303. (404)681-2900

Sid and Marty Krofft are fifth-generation puppeteers who have expanded their business to television shows and the production and design of rides, shows, and attractions for major theme parks. The World of Sid and Marty Krofft is built within a nine-story building, and contains several colorful fantasy shows and a few unusual rides. One of these rides is the "Giant Pinball Machine," in which riders climb into oversized pinballs that are shot into the huge machine, careening and banging against bumpers, flippers, and scoring holes. This is one of the more unusual of the attraction parks.

HAWAII

SEA LIFE PARK; Makapuu, Honolulu, Hawaii (808)259-7933

Owned and operated by Lion Country Safari, Inc., Sea Life Park offers the same fine oceanographic attractions as the Sea World and Marineland parks.

ILLINOIS

ADVENTURELAND; Lake Street near Medinah, Addison, Il. 60101. (312)529-8880

Located east of Chicago on the Eisenhower Expressway, Adventureland acquired many of the rides from Riverview Park when it closed down, except for the roller coasters.

OLD CHICAGO; 555 S. Bolingbrook Dr., Bolingbrook, Il. 60439. (312)759-1895

Old Chicago is the world's first major indoor shopping center/amusement park, with hundreds of stores, restaurants, shows, games, and rides, including the "Corkscrew." It is located 35 miles southwest of the Chicago

The shopping area of Old Chicago.

Loop at the intersection of Interstate 55 and Illinois Highway 53, and is open every day of the year.

MARRIOTT'S GREAT AMERICA; Gurnee, Il. 60031. (312)249–2020

The superbly produced and highly entertaining shows of the Great America parks include the Theatre Royale, with Bugs Bunny and the Warner Brothers gang, the Grand Music Hall, an elaborate musical revue, and the Snowshoe Saloon, with musical comedy in an 1890s frontier atmosphere. The rides include "The Columbia"—a double-decker carousel, the "Turn-of-the-Century"—a super corkscrew coaster—and the Sky-Whirl—the world's first triple Ferris wheel.

INDIANA

INDIANA BEACH; Lake Shafer, Monticello, Indiana 47960. (219)583–4141

An attractive amusement area set out in the middle of Lake Shafer, Indiana Beach is complete with camping, boat rides, water ski shows, motels, restaurants, shops, and over 20 rides.

World War I fighters in Pontchartrain Beach Amusement Park.

ENCHANTED FOREST; Mounted Route Box 386, Chesterton, Indiana 46304. (219)926–1614

Enchanted Forest is beautifully situated within a grove of old oak trees, with plenty of public and private picnic space and forty rides and attractions.

IOWA

ARNOLD'S PARK; Arnold's Park, Iowa 51331. (712)332–5658

Located on Lake Okoboji, "one of three natural blue lakes in the world," Arnold's Park offers dancing in the Roof Garden Ballroom, scenic tours over the lake, and plenty of rides. The park began in the 1870s.

RIVERVIEW PARK; 8th and Corning, Des Moines, Iowa 50313. (515)288–3621

Riverview Park began in the 1860's as a picnic grove, and although it has blossomed into a well-equipped amusement park, the quiet, woodsy atmosphere still remains.

Six Flags Over Mid-America.

The Pirate Ship *Victrix* in
Worlds Of Fun.

The Garden of Marvels in Great Adventure.

KANSAS

JOYLAND AMUSEMENT PARK; 2801 South Hillside, Wichita, Kansas 67216. (316)684–0179

Joyland Park is the biggest and boldest traditional amusement park in Kansas, containing a Frontier Town, Mother Goose Gardens, roller skating, miniature golf, swimming, and a huge, swift roller coaster which gives you a broad but brief view of the Kansas plains.

KENTUCKY

BEECH BEND PARK; Bowling Green, Kentucky 42101. (502) 842–8101

Beech Bend Park is a combination campground, picnic ground, zoo, and amusement park, making it one of the most complete recreation areas in the nation. There are over 6,500 campsites, 35 rides, horse stables, a raceway, a go-cart track, nature trails, and a swimming pool. Beech Bend Park makes a fun and very inexpensive family vacation spot.

LOUISIANA

PONCHARTRAIN BEACH AMUSEMENT PARK; Elysian Fields Avenue and Lakeshore Dr., New Orleans, La. 70122. (504)288–1421

In New Orleans the action is at either of two places, Bourbon Street in the French Quarter, or Pontchartrain Beach. Set on the shores of Lake

*The Comet of Crystal Beach
Amusement Park.*

Pontchartrain, the park has a huge
assortment of rides, attractions, and
games, and is tied with Miracle Strip
as the best traditional amusement
park in the South.

MARYLAND

PLAYLAND AMUSEMENT PARK;
65th Street, Ocean City, Md.
21842. (301)289–8353

Playland is another of the seaside
amusement parks, with lots of rides,
games, and fun.

MARSHALL HALL AMUSEMENT
PARK; Route 227, Bryans
Road, Md. 20616. (301)743–5575

Located across the Potomac River
from Mount Vernon, Marshall Hall is
a lovely and fun family park with spacious picnic grounds. The best way to
get there is by the Wilson Boat Line,
which sails down the Potomac from
Washington, D.C.

MASSACHUSETTS

LINCOLN PARK; Route 195, North
Dartmouth, Mass. 02747.
(617)999–6984

This is a fine New England park that
not only has a large assortment of the

usual traditional amusements, but also a golf driving range and two athletic fields. Like all of the parks in New England, Lincoln Park is open during the summer only.

RIVERSIDE PARK; Route 159, Agawam, Mass. 01001. (413)737–1438

Riverside Park started in 1940 on the ruins of an older trolley park which a movie theater owner hoped to revive. Amazingly he did so. Riverside Park is the best amusement park in New England, with over 35 rides and stockcar racing on the Riverside Park Speedway.

PARAGON PARK; 175 Nantasket Ave., Hull, Mass. 02045. (617) 925–0115

Paragon Park is located just south of Boston on Nantasket Beach and contains lots of excitement with over 40 rides, including what was for many years the world's highest and longest roller coaster. The park has a nice miniature golf course and lots of fun and games.

WHALOM PARK; Route 13, Lunenburg, Mass. 01462. (617)342–3707.

A very popular New England lakeside summer resort, Whalom Park is a charming traditional amusement park, and there are plenty of water sports and activities available on Lake Whalom.

MICHIGAN

BOB-LO ISLAND; Detroit, Mich. 48226. (313)962–9622

Ferry boats or steam boats departing from downtown Detroit or neighbor-

ing Windsor, Ontario, take visitors to Bob-Lo, which started in the 1880s. The amusements on this unique island are various, ranging from swanboat rides and antique cars to a log flume and the new "Thunderbolt" roller coaster. This is certainly one of the most beautifully set amusement parks in the United States, and makes for a full, relaxing, and fun-packed day. The boatrides to the island are half the fun.

EDGEWATER PARK; 23500 West Seven Mile Road, Detroit, Mich. 48219. (313)731–2660

Although it has some rough competition from Bob-Lo Island, Edgewater Park is holding its own as another of the carefully preserved turn-of-the-century amusement parks.

MINNESOTA

VALLEYFAIR; One Valleyfair Drive, Shakopee, Minn. 55379. (612) 445–7600

Valleyfair's single theme is highly original and attractively simple: a turn-of-the-century trolley park. While not in the league of the big theme parks, Valleyfair's beauty and charm more than cover for its size. The fifty rides, shows, and attractions include trolley cars which clang their way through the park, an old mill, an antique carousel, a vaudeville house, an old-fashioned ice cream parlor, and many more, within a woodsy 1900 setting. The only major amusement park in Minnesota, Valleyfair is located southwest of Minneapolis on Highway 101.

MISSOURI

SIX FLAGS OVER MID-AMERICA;
Eureka, Missouri 63025.
(314)938–5300

Located west of St. Louis on Interstate 44, this is the third of the Six Flags parks. In its six sections it contains a runaway mine train through a Missouri forest, a log flume ride, and The Palace, a tribute to the St. Louis Exhibition of 1904. Its brand-new "Screamin' Eagle" roller coaster is the highest and longest in the world.

FAIRYLAND PARK; 7501 Prospect
Ave., Kansas City, Mo. 64132.
(816)333–2040

Fairyland Park is one of the best traditional amusement parks in the Midwest. It is spotless and well managed, and has over 35 rides.

WORLDS OF FUN; 4545 Worlds of
Fun Avenue, Kansas City, Mo.
64161. (816)454–4545

This theme park is divided into Africa, Americana, Scandinavia, and the Orient. The Tivoli Music Hall presents some great shows, and the entertainment is almost endless with two more theater shows, puppet shows, dolphin shows, and a petting farm. And of course there are lots of wild theme rides.

NEBRASKA

PEONY PARK; 81st and Cass Streets,
Omaha, Nebraska 68114.
(402)391–6253

As the only amusement park in the state, Peony Park has some nice picnic areas, as well as swimming, dancing, an athletic field, miniature golf, and rides.

NEW HAMPSHIRE

CANOBIE LAKE PARK; Salem, N.H.
03079. (603)893–3506

Located 35 miles north of Boston off U.S. 93, Canobie Lake Park offers a huge selection of amusements and water activities on the lake.

NEW JERSEY

CLEMENTON LAKE PARK; Route
534, Clementon, N.J. 08021.
(609)783–0263

Rides, games, a penny arcade, and a stern-wheel boat ride over the lake make up the fun at this traditional amusement park that grew out of a picnic grove over a century ago.

BERTRAND ISLAND PARK; Mt. Arlington, N.J. 07856. (201)398–
0136

This fine park is ideal for group outings, as it is on an island and therefore easy to keep the group together. Bertrand Island has plenty of picnic space, water sports, and over 25 rides.

MARINE PIER, PLAYLAND,
SPORTLAND PIER, CASINO
ARCADE PIER, HUNT'S
PIER, SURF SIDE PIER; all located on the Boardwalk, Wildwood, N.J. 08260.

All six of these amusement piers are separately owned, but because they are all within just a few feet of each other, they can be viewed as one amusement area. Together these six piers combine to make Wildwood one of the most fun and enjoyable places to spend a summer day and evening, or an entire summer vacation. The beach is great, and the amusements are endless.

SEASIDE HEIGHTS CASINO, PIER, AND POOL, Grant and Boardwalk, Seaside Heights, N.J. 08751. (201)793-6488

This is another of the many fun amusement piers in New Jersey, with 45 major and kiddie rides and a large penny arcade.

GREAT ADVENTURE; Jackson, N.J. 08527. (201)928-2000

Great Adventure is divided between what is the largest drive-through safari park outside of Africa, and the Enchanted Forest theme park. The Enchanted Forest is in turn divided into Dream Street, Strawberry Fair, Neptune's Kingdom, and Rootin' Tootin' Rip Roarin'. One section of Dream Street is the Garden of Marvels, which is a landscaped garden featuring a 1/25 scale of 76 famous European buildings, ships, and trains. There is a pay-one-price policy for the Safari alone, the Enchanted Forest alone, or the Enchanted Forest and Safari together.

NEW YORK

ASTROLAND; 1000 Surf Ave., Brooklyn, N.Y. 11224. (212)372-0275

On good old Coney Island itself, Astroland contains Coney Island's newest rides and attractions. The park is right across 10th Street from the Cyclone.

CRYSTAL BEACH AMUSEMENT PARK; Buffalo, N.Y. 14207. (416)894-1642

Beautiful Crystal Beach is actually in Ontario, Canada, across the Peace Bridge from Buffalo, but more Americans make use of it than Canadians, and there is no doubt that it is after all a traditional American amusement park. There is a fine bathing beach, plenty of picnic space, and a huge assortment of rides, including one of the world's best roller coasters, the "Comet."

The "Dragon Coaster" in Playland, Rye, N.Y.

Carowinds.

Geauga Lake Park's Big Ditch.

The Antique Cars of Idora Park.

ROSELAND PARK; Lake Shore Drive, Canandaigua, N.Y. 14424. (315)394–1140

Roseland Park is another of the lakeside amusement parks, with a wide assortment of rides, games, and water sports on Lake Canadaigua.

GASLIGHT VILLAGE; Route 9, Lake George, N.Y. 12845. (518)792–8227

This theme park takes you back to the Gay Nineties, with several museums and lots of fun turn-of-the-century rides and shows, including some great vaudeville and melodrama in the Opera House. The Cavalcade of Cars Museum alone is worth the visit.

STORYTOWN, U.S.A.; Route 9, Lake George, N.Y. 12845. (518)792–8802

Owned and run by Gaslight Village, Storytown is an enchanting family fairyland, with rides, storybook gardens, acrobatic and sea-life shows, a ghost town, and a trip through Jungle Land.

PLAYLAND; Rye, N.Y. 10580. (914)967-2040

This is the "perfectly planned" amusement park that catered to the family when it was built in 1926. Through careful management and attention by the Westchester County Commission, Playland has remained a beautiful and fun family park, with boatrides over the Long Island Sound and nightly musical entertainment.

DREAMLAND PARK-SEA BREEZE; 4600 Culver Road, Rochester, N.Y. 14624. (716)467-3422

Located on Lake Ontario, Dreamland Park is one of those vintage amusement parks with a surprising amount of the vintage atmosphere and rides, including one of the few surviving mill chute rides.

OLYMPIC PARK; 1300 Scottsville Road, Rochester, N.Y. 14624. (716)436-9180

Olympic Park is basically an attraction park, and is loaded with family fun, including Mississippi River Steamboat rides, a Bavarian beer garden, and a Frontier Village.

ROCKAWAY'S PLAYLAND; 185 Beach 97th Street, Rockaway Beach, N.Y. 11693. (212)945-7000

Located on Rockaway Beach on Long Island, Rockaway's Playland is somewhat small, but very attractive and lots of fun. It is famous for its Most Beautiful Baby Contest, as well as the "Atom Smasher," the roller coaster which was "ridden" by moviegoers all over the world in the 1951 film *This Is Cinerama*. Like the Coney Island parks, Rockaway is the gathering place for many on a hot New York summer day.

NORTH CAROLINA

THE LAND OF OZ; Banner Elk, N.C. 28604. (704)387-2231

"Dorothy" takes you down the yellow brick road through the Land of Oz in this pleasant family theme park. Along the way, the various characters of *The Wizard of Oz* greet and entertain you, and join you on the way to the Emerald City. This park is a must for families with small children.

CAROWINDS; Interstate 77, Charlotte, N.C. 28210. (704)588-2600

Carowinds is split up into seven sections, each one depicting a facet of the 300 years of Carolina heritage. There is Plantation Square, Queen's Colony, Country Crossroads, Indian Thicket, Pirate Island, Frontier Outpost, and Contemporary Carolina. There is the usual assortment of theme rides, circus acts, magic shows, and different types of musical presentations.

The Catawba Stern-wheeler of Cedar Point Park.

OHIO

GEAUGA LAKE PARK; Route 43, Aurora, Ohio 44202. (216)562-7131

Geauga Lake Park is a century-old trolley park which through constant renovation, change, and addition (to the tune of $1,000,000 per year for the last five years) has by this time become an extremely attractive modern park. An impressive feat, and the variety of amusements and entertainment at Geauga Lake is no less impressive, numbering over 50. Geauga Lake Park is another example of successful and imaginative management.

SEA WORLD OF OHIO; Sea World Drive, Aurora, Ohio 44202. (216)562-8101

This is the newest venture by Sea World, Inc., offering the same superb sea life entertainment. It is located across the lake from Geauga Lake Park.

CHIPPEWA LAKE; Chippewa Lake, Ohio 44215. (216)769-2481

Located on a 385-acre lake, Chippewa Lake has plenty of rides, games, food, and amusement park fun.

LE SOURDSVILLE LAKE AMUSEMENT PARK; Middletown, Ohio 45043. (606)539-7339

Located just south of Middletown, Le Sourdsville Lake is another fine lakeside amusement park, with the standard traditional fun and games, including the Indy 500, a racetrack version of the bumper cars.

Kings Island.

*Mary Tudor Square marks
the entrance to Hersheypark.*

IDORA PARK; Route 62, Youngstown, Ohio 44511. (216)782–1161

Idora Park is astounding in how beautiful and clean it is, which is no small
feat when an amusement park is
pushing 100 years old. Through excellent management, pride, and care,
this fine traditional park has maintained a high standard of beauty
and fun comparable to Denver's Lakeside Park. The park abounds in greenery, the rides are good, there is a large
kiddie section set off by itself, and the
"Wildcat" roller coaster (one of two in
the park) is one of the nation's most
exciting and fastest coasters. The residents of Youngstown should be
proud.

KINGS ISLAND; 6600 Kings Island
Dr., Kings Mills, Ohio 45034.
(606)628–2464

Located just north of Cincinnati,
Kings Island is my favorite choice of
all the big theme parks. Centered
around the Eiffel Tower are International Street, Oktoberfest, Lion Country Safari, Coney Island, Rivertown,
and The Happy Land of Hanna-Barbera. The big, bold, and colorful Kings
Island is easily one of the best family
entertainment packages in the nation.

CEDAR POINT PARK; Sandusky,
Ohio 44870. (419)626–0830

To see Cedar Point now, it is difficult
to believe that this magnificent traditional amusement park was, in the
1950s, run-down, and headed for an almost certain closing. At that time it
was bought by a new company which
poured incredible amounts of money
into it to make it the largest and by
far the best traditional amusement
park in the nation. Cedar Point Park
is located on a peninsula on Lake Erie
just north of Sandusky, with a marina

The Thunderbolt roller
coaster of Kennywood Park.

Opryland, U.S.A.

on the west side and a nice bathing beach on the east side, including a trailer park and the gorgeously renovated Hotel Breakers. The amusement park itself contains America's largest collection of rides and attractions, from a Frontier Trail of pioneer heritage, arts, and crafts, to a sky tower offering a breathtaking view of Lake Erie, to four roller coasters, to a "San Francisco Earthquake" ride (originally from Freedomland, U.S.A.). With its excellent amusements, accommodations, restaurants, and water sports, it is easy to spend several days at Cedar Point.

OKLAHOMA

SPRINGLAKE AMUSEMENT PARK; 1800 Springlake Drive, Oklahoma City, Okla. 73111. (405)424-1405

Springlake Park is another of the vintage turn-of-the-century amusement parks, with plenty of old-fashioned amusement park fun, from guess-your-weight to a Haunted House dark ride to bumper cars to a fun house. It is a well-kept-up park.

BELL'S AMUSEMENT PARK; 21st & New Haven, Tulsa, Okla. 74114. (918)932-1991

The gardening, grounds, and maintenance division should be applauded for keeping Bell's one of the most beautiful traditional amusement parks in the nation. There isn't a scrap of paper to be seen, flowers bloom everywhere, and the grounds themselves are paved entirely with brick. There are over 27 rides and plenty of games. Bell's is located on the Oklahoma State Fairgrounds, of which it becomes a part during the fair days, although it is open by itself daily from May 1 through Labor Day.

OREGON

THE OAKS AMUSEMENT PARK; East end of Sellwood Bridge, Portland, Ore. 97202. (503)233-5777

This fine traditional park opened in 1905 to coincide with the Lewis and Clark World's Fair of that year. Since then it has continued to offer spacious picnic grounds and plenty of rides and games. It is the only major park in Oregon.

PENNSYLVANIA

DORNEY PARK; 3830 Dorney Park Road, Allentown, Pa. 18104. (215)395-3724

Built in 1884, Dorney Park is another example of excellent management and upkeep in traditional American amusement parks. The fascinating thing about Dorney is its atmosphere, which is an intoxicating mixture of relaxing picnic grove and excitement-packed Coney Island. This atmosphere, the beauty, the many fun rides (including a mill-chute, an Indy 500 bumper-cars, and a fantastic coaster), and the fine eating make Dorney Park one of the very finest traditional amusement parks in the nation.

SIX GUN TERRITORY; Easton & Moreland Roads, Willow Grove, Pa. 19090. (215)659-8000

As obvious by its title, Six Gun Territory is an Old West theme park, with saloon shows, stage shows, gunfights, and several rides.

CONNEAUT LAKE PARK; Conneaut Lake, Pa. 16316. (814)382–5115

Located in northwestern Pennsylvania, Conneaut Lake Park makes a very relaxing and fun summer resort, with amusements, fishing, golfing, boating, swimming, and entertainment. There are plenty of accommodations available during the summer.

HERSHEYPARK; Hershey, Pa. 17033. (717)534–3900

This theme park is a must-see for anyone near the area. Besides the rides and shows, one section of the park is devoted to crafts shops operated by the Pennsylvania Dutch. Chocolate World is located outside the main entrance to the park and is free.

WEST VIEW PARK; West View, Pittsburgh, Pa. 15229. (412)931–3700

Located just north of downtown Pittsburgh, West View Park is another of the great Pennsylvania trolley parks which to this day has not slipped one bit in popularity. Its expansive picnic grounds are supplemented by over 30 rides, including 3 roller coasters (one of which is a racer). This is another one of the great eastern parks in which the serene woodsy picnic setting and the vintage rides and attractions make you believe that at the end of the day you'll be walking back to your Model T Ford.

KENNYWOOD PARK; 4800 Kennywood Blvd., West Mifflin, Pa. 15122. (412)461–0500

Located on a bluff overlooking the Monongahela River just south of Pittsburgh, Kennywood Park is Pennsylvania's largest traditional park and one of the most thrilling in the nation. If you like roller coasters, Kennywood Park is for you. It has five of them, one of which (the Thunderbolt) achieved nationwide fame when roller-coaster expert Bob Cartmell rated it number one in his list of the top ten coasters in the world. Besides its coasters, Kennywood has everything else under the sun, including a Pennsylvania Dutch Grove and Noah's Ark. Something new is introduced each year.

RHODE ISLAND

ROCKY POINT PARK; Warwick Neck, R.I. 02889. (401)737–8000

This is Rhode Island's biggest and best park, located on Narragansett Bay. It has an Olympic-sized salt-water swimming pool, miniature golf, and lots of rides, and the Rocky Point Shore Dinner Hall serves delicious seafood dinners.

TENNESSEE

OPRYLAND, U.S.A.; Nashville, Tenn. 37214. (615)889–6600

Opryland's star attraction is, of course, the Opry House, the new home of the Grand Ole Opry. The Grand Ole Opry is now more popular than ever before, and tickets to see the fantastic musical shows must be reserved well in advance, several months ahead of time for the summer. Otherwise, there is plenty of music in Opryland itself, from country to jazz to pop to show tunes. For reservations for the Grand Ole Opry, write: Grand Ole Opry Ticket Office, 2800 Opryland Drive, Nashville, Tenn. 37214

LAKE WINNEPESAUKAH; Chattanooga, Tenn. 30741. (404)866-5681

A beautiful amusement park with a country atmosphere, Lake Winnepesaukah has plenty of rides, games, and picnic facilities, as well as water sports available on the lake.

TEXAS

STATE FAIR PARK; Dallas, Texas 75226. (214)823-9931

The home of the Texas State Fair and the Cotton Bowl, State Fair Park was one of the first fairs in the nation to begin operating as a permanent midway, besides the sixteen-day run of the fair. There are over 36 rides, and special shows are always being presented in the music hall.

SIX FLAGS OVER TEXAS; 2201 Road to Six Flags, Arlington, Texas 76010. (817)261-2771

This is the theme park that started the big boom of theme parks. Located halfway between Fort Worth and Dallas, Six Flags Over Texas has more rides, shows, and attractions than ever before. Highly entertaining musical revues are presented in the Southern Palace and the Crazy Horse Saloon, as well as Sid and Marty Krofft's Puppet Theatre, a dolphin show, a petting zoo and, in short, enough entertainment to last from opening to closing time.

ASTROWORLD, U.S.A.; 9001 Kirby Drive, Houston, Texas 77001. (713)743-4500

Now owned by Six Flags, Inc., Astroworld contains a sleigh ride through the Alps, water bumper-boats, and plenty of other rides, attractions, shows, and big-name entertainment spaced throughout the park's ten theme sections: Americana Square, Mod Ville, Alpine Valley, European Village, Western Junction, Children's World, Plaza De Fiesta, Oriental Corner, Country Fair, and Coney Island.

LION COUNTRY SAFARI; 601 Lion Country Parkway, Grand Prairie, Texas 75050. (214)263-2201

Located just a few miles from Six Flags Over Texas, this is the third of the Lion Country Safari parks.

UTAH

LAGOON; Interstate 15, Utah 84101. (801)363-4451

Located midway between Salt Lake City and Ogden, Lagoon is one of those older amusement parks which through constant renovation somewhat resembles a modern theme park, although it is basically traditional. Its biggest attraction is the Lagoon Opera House, where the University of Utah Players present current musical plays. The park also has a huge swimming pool, miniature golf, nearby camping, and plenty of thrilling rides, with an old-fashioned fun house.

*A Main Street parade in
Astroworld, U.S.A.*

VIRGINIA

KINGS DOMINION; Ashland, Va.
23005. (804)798–4761

Kings Dominion is similar to the original Kings Island and, believe it or not, actually just a little bit better. Around its Eiffel Tower are International Street, the Happy Land of Hanna-Barbera, Lion Country Safari, Coney Island, and Old Virginia. It is located 23 miles north of Richmond on Interstate 95.

LAKESIDE AMUSEMENT PARK;
1526 E. Main St., Salem, Va.
24153. (703)366–8871

Lakeside Park is a fine and well-equipped traditional park in a country setting, with plenty of picnic facilities and lots of rides, including an exceptionally speedy "Shooting Star" roller coaster.

THE OLD COUNTRY; Williamsburg,
Va. 23185. (804)220–1510.

As the third and newest of the Busch Gardens parks, The Old Country is split up into Germany, England, and France, with a Rhine riverboat cruise in Germany, a medieval garden and the Globe Theatre with a Shakespearean play in England, and a Le Mans speedway, a French Alps log flume, and Three Musketeers theater with trained animals in France.

WASHINGTON

FUN FOREST AMUSEMENT
PARK; 370 Thomas Street,
Seattle, Wash. 98109. (206)624–
1585

As the only major amusement park in Washington, Fun Forest is located in Seattle Center, the grounds for the 1962 Seattle World's Fair. There are plenty of rides and games, as well as many exhibits and shows on the lovely and still active fairgrounds.

WISCONSIN

DANDELION PARK; Muskego, Wisconsin 53105. (414)679–2400

Located just outside of Milwaukee, Dandelion Park is the biggest amusement park in the state, with rides, games, and excellent picnic facilities.

Index

256